MW01627670

GOLDEN STEER STEAKHOUSE LAS VEGAS
Est. 1958

Recipes, Tales & Celebrities from the Legendary Las Vegas Restaurant

James O. Fraioli
with Golden Steer Steakhouse Proprietor Dr. Michael J. Signorelli

Foreword by Carolyn G. Goodman, Mayor of Las Vegas, Nevada
Food Photography by Tucker + Hossler

WILLOW CREEK PRESS®

Published by Willow Creek Press, Inc.
P.O. Box 147, Minocqua, Wisconsin 54548

Designed By Donnie Rubo

ISBN: 978-1-62343-987-3

First Edition: September 2017

10 9 8 7 6 5 4 3 2 1

Printed in China

To all the guests of the Golden Steer Steakhouse, both past and present.
Thank you for your patronage…
And to the past, present, and future employees
for making the Steer so special.

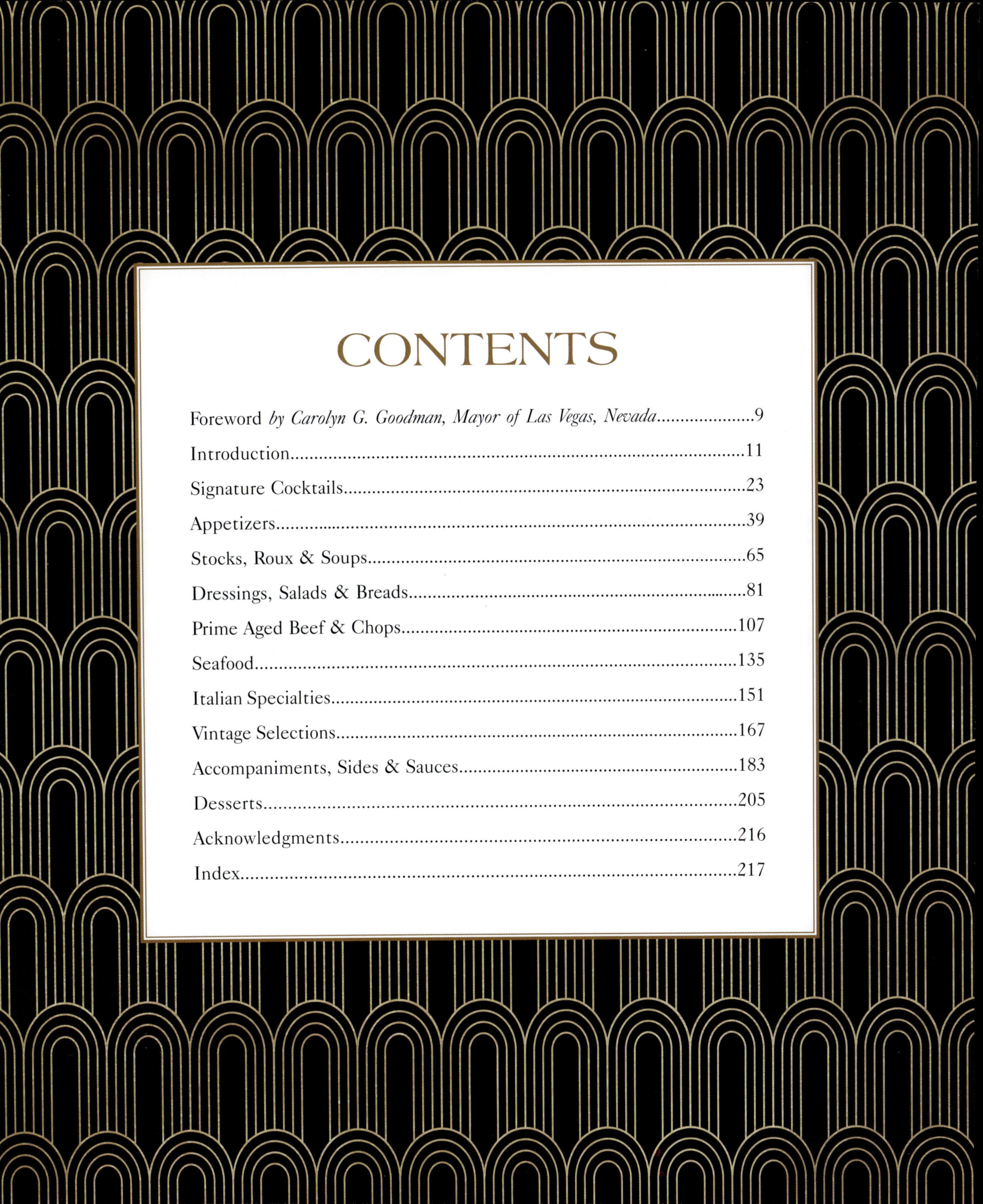

CONTENTS

Foreword *by Carolyn G. Goodman, Mayor of Las Vegas, Nevada* 9

Introduction 11

Signature Cocktails 23

Appetizers 39

Stocks, Roux & Soups 65

Dressings, Salads & Breads 81

Prime Aged Beef & Chops 107

Seafood 135

Italian Specialties 151

Vintage Selections 167

Accompaniments, Sides & Sauces 183

Desserts 205

Acknowledgments 216

Index 217

GOLDEN NUGGET
GAMBLING HALL
LUCKY STRIKE
BINGO
GOLDEN NUGGET
SALOON
GOLDEN NUGGET
1905
Rexall
DRUGS
HALL
BINGO
HOTEL
SAL SAGEV
LAS VEGAS CLUB
BOULDER
CLUB
NO MINIMUM

FOREWORD

by Carolyn G. Goodman, Mayor of Las Vegas, Nevada

By way of introduction, I am Carolyn Goodman. I am the mayor of Las Vegas. My husband, Oscar Goodman, also served as mayor from 1999 to 2011.

Las Vegas is known worldwide as the Entertainment Capital of the World. You can only imagine what a thrill it is to serve the city as its ambassador on the international stage. We offer what I believe is the best the planet has in shows, clubs, attractions, and restaurants. We encompass every aspect of entertainment.

On the lighter side of being mayor, and as part of my "official" duties, I have the pleasure of visiting many restaurants, ribbon cuttings, proclamations, business functions, convention parties, and special events. Having to wine and dine at the best restaurants in the world is truly a labor of love.

My husband, Oscar, after serving three terms as mayor, had become so addicted to his "work" that he opened his own restaurant, Oscar's, which serves "Beef, Booze and Broads" downtown. As much as we enjoy his restaurant, we also venture out to visit one of our favorite dining establishments, the Golden Steer Steakhouse.

The Steer is legendary for its prime steaks and many tableside preparations, and also for the A-list celebrities who have frequented the restaurant. Oscar can vouch for some of the infamous guests to visit the Steer. Prior to being mayor, he was widely known as the mob lawyer, representing many notorious gangsters over the span of his career.

I would be amiss not to mention that Dr. Michael J. Signorelli, the proprietor, is a good, personal friend of mine, and has been for many years. When he purchased the Golden Steer Steakhouse in 2001, I knew the restaurant would be in great hands. There is always the fear that when new owners step in, their next move is to make changes. This was definitely not the case with Dr. Signorelli. He has steadfastly maintained the integrity of its history, from the menu to the last drop of the classic cocktails.

The Golden Steer Steakhouse has been the standard-bearer of a first-class steak house for more than fifty-five years. To prevail and be recognized as a classic restaurant over the decades is testimony itself to the greatness of the Golden Steer Steakhouse, its owner, and its staff.

INTRODUCTION

For those of us who cherish the art of dining, our first mission after arriving in any new city is to ask, "Where do the locals eat?" If you ask any Las Vegas bartender, concierge, cabdriver, front-desk associate, restaurant wait staff, or seasoned local, the Golden Steer Steakhouse will receive a knowing nod of approval. The Steer has been the epitome of a classic steakhouse since opening its doors in 1958. It is the oldest continually operating restaurant in the city of Las Vegas.

Since the beginning, the Golden Steer Steakhouse has prided itself on serving beautifully marbled, prime, dry-aged beef, butchered in-house. It is one of the few restaurants in Las Vegas where the prime beef served is certified prime-grade. The Steer offers classic food in generous portions reminiscent of another era. This is a restaurant where you can leave your expectations for nouvelle cuisine at the door.

Although Las Vegas has experienced many makeovers throughout the years, and many restaurants have come and gone, the Golden Steer Steakhouse has remained virtually unchanged since its inception while continuing to be a model of quality and consistency, led by proprietor Dr. Michael J. Signorelli. The longevity and experience of the staff have been the heart of this legendary restaurant. The majority of employees, front and back of the house, have been at the Steer for an average of thirty-five years. The talented executive chef Sergio Medina, for example, has been working the kitchen for thirty-eight years. Waiter Fabian Ong has been serving guests for the last forty years. And general manager and partner John E. Burke began busing tables at the Golden Steer Steakhouse in 1983 at the age of eighteen. Johnny, as he's called, along with the other Steer staff, exemplifies the classic American success story. As the old-timers retire, second and third generations of their families follow in their footsteps. This has enabled the Golden Steer Steakhouse to maintain its consistently great service and high quality of food. It has also allowed the Steer to maintain its reputation as one of the best restaurants in Las Vegas. Recently, Mayor Carolyn Goodman proclaimed April 7 as Golden Steer Steakhouse Day.

Truly everyone who is anyone in the past five and a half decades of Las Vegas history has been seated in one of the dark wood and red leather banquettes at the Golden Steer Steakhouse,

surrounded by western art and artifacts, including an odd portrait of one late beloved regular, *Magnificent Seven* star Charles Bronson.

As you enter through the etched-glass doors into the softly lit restaurant, the classic long bar beckons to your left. Chandelier light fixtures, red velvet wallpaper, and a grand piano add to the vintage atmosphere. It is Grandma's parlor, with booze. The lounge ambience begs you to indulge in a classic martini, made with gin in the old days. Chilled, up, "no fruit," just the way Dean Martin ordered it. The Steer is not just a restaurant of fond memory, it is where locals go to make memories. It is where old school goes to get schooled. The dining room is encircled by mahogany-and-leather banquettes. The crisp white tablecloths and napkins are simply illuminated with a candle. The classic songs of Frank Sinatra and fellow crooners waft through the air. Dean Martin, Sammy Davis Jr., Elvis, Joe DiMaggio, Marilyn Monroe, Howard Hughes, Muhammad Ali, Natalie Wood, Betty Grable, Mickey Rooney, Bette Midler, John Wayne, legendary mobsters... they've all dined at the Golden Steer Steakhouse, and most are recognized today with personalized booths. In fact, guests can enjoy a delicious dinner in the very seat where a legend once sat.

While the tuxedoed staff, consummate professionals, many of them here their entire careers, watchfully tend to your every need, you can indulge in the same dishes that some of America's most famous enjoyed: Clams Casino, Escargots de Bourgogne, and the classic Italian starter Toasted Ravioli with house-made Marinara Sauce, followed by fresh Dover Sole, hand-cut prime steaks, and impressive tableside flambés for dessert. Without question, this place has a neighborhood at-home feel about it... and that's why the Golden Steer Steakhouse remains popular with locals, vacationers, as well as the rich and famous today. Racecar legend Mario Andretti, actor Nicolas Cage, former Playboy bunny Holly Madison, local ventriloquist Terry Fator... they all still dine at the Steer.

Now the long-awaited cookbook is finally here, loaded with the Steer's signature cocktails and delicious, easy-to-make comfort foods accompanied by a bevy of selected wines. Before it was vogue, the staff of the Golden Steer Steakhouse promoted eating organic produce and sustainable meats and seafood whenever possible. Now they reveal their prized recipes that display their commitment to flavorful dishes of superior quality. The Golden Steer Steakhouse never cuts corners while incorporating traditional and Old World techniques into every meal.

A Trip Down Memory Lane

In 1959, the New Frontier Hotel was located two blocks south of the Golden Steer Steakhouse on the famous Las Vegas Strip. The employees, stagehands, lounge acts, and headliners of the hotel would flock to the Steer for the "Night Owl specials," wind-down beverages, and camaraderie. The biggest seller: the half-pound hamburger with fries and a twelve-ounce draft beer, all for just $2.95. One of the headliners, a quiet, unassuming, good-looking singer, always came in to order the burger and fries, but with a soda instead of a beer. He performed only sixty-nine shows in the small theater at the New Frontier, to half-full showrooms. His venue was soon canceled.

Ten years later, that same headliner returned to perform in the two-thousand-seat showroom at the International Hotel. He performed 629 shows to sold-out audiences. At the time, one in two visitors to Las Vegas would attend his performance. And like clockwork, he would always visit his old haunt, the Golden Steer Steakhouse. Unfortunately, the hamburger was no longer on the menu. Instead, the chefs in the back would hand-chop a sirloin steak to make into a hamburger. It was then served to the singer with his usual fries and a soda. This time, he was seated at a banquette named after him. The name on the brass plaque, as it appears today: ELVIS PRESLEY.

Around the same time, indomitable "Yankee Clipper" and future Baseball Hall of Famer Joe DiMaggio was another frequent guest at the Golden Steer Steakhouse. He was the first sports star to become a nationally recognized celebrity. Mr. DiMaggio loved the action that Las Vegas offered. He soon married a movie star who would become a legend in her own right, Marilyn Monroe. Today Mr. DiMaggio has two booths with his name on plaques at the Steer. As the story goes, Marilyn Monroe introduced Mr. DiMaggio to the Golden Steer Steakhouse in the 1960s. The two always sat in Booth 3, a corner booth in the main dining room, and Mr. DiMaggio always ordered roses for their table before Marilyn's arrival. They would share a Caesar salad and the Châteaubriand, both prepared tableside as they still are today, then split a Cherries Jubilee flambé, also prepared tableside, for dessert. After Marilyn's untimely death, Mr. DiMaggio continued to dine at the Steer when he was in Vegas, but now sat at a banquette in a side dining room, out of sight and away from the memories of Booth 3.

Through the years, the Golden Steer Steakhouse gained legendary status, thanks especially to the loyal patronage of the Rat Pack. In the late 1960s, one of Las Vegas's less publicized paradoxes was that the city was still in the throes of segregation. African Americans were not welcome in casinos, bars, or restaurants. They were not allowed to use the swimming pools and certainly not permitted to stay at the hotel. This was quite an enigma as most of the lounge performers, groups, bands, and orchestras in the pit at that time were predominantly black: the Four Tops, Smokey Robinson, the Temptations, and the Drifters, to name a few. The original Rat Pack—Frank Sinatra, Peter Lawford, Joey Bishop, Dean Martin, and Sammy Davis Jr.—performed at the Sands Hotel. At the end of their shows, they would have to leave, as Sammy Davis Jr. was not permitted to stay at the Sands. Along with other black entertainers, Mr. Davis would check in at the interracial Moulin Rouge Hotel on Bonanza Avenue, just north of the city limits. The Golden Steer Steakhouse at the time was located on San Francisco Street (now Sahara Avenue), the border between the city and the county of Las Vegas. The restaurant was just a few blocks from the Sands, so it was conveniently located and en route to the Moulin Rouge. The Rat Pack, on their way to the Steer, would always have an extensive entourage in tow, fondly known as the Rat Pack Mascots: Angie Dickinson, Juliet Prowse, Buddy Greco, Shirley MacLaine, and comedian Corbett Monica, who frequently worked as the opening act for Frank Sinatra. The Golden Steer Steakhouse menu offered Italian food for Frank and "Dino," and there was a wide variety of prime beef and steaks

Elvis Presley's

to satisfy the appetite of the rest of the Pack. The bonus was that the Steer had a piano in the lounge (it's still here today). Even after performing, which was twice nightly in those days, the Rat Pack loved to entertain, and belted out songs to the delight of all until the wee hours of the morning.

In these early days, the Golden Steer Steakhouse was also known as a hangout for some of Las Vegas's more nefarious characters. It is no secret that the Founding Fathers of the casino and hotel industry in Las Vegas were connected to the Mafia. On the occasions when they dined at the Steer, they would always be given Dining Room A, the room simply known to Steer employees as the Mob Room. Today, this room still serves guests requesting privacy. This private room also offered one distinct advantage not available at other restaurants in town: It had a secret door. This door led from the dining room to the back of a service bar then through another door to the alley at the rear of the restaurant. It provided complete exclusivity and safe passage for these cautious diners and their entourages. In Martin Scorsese's film *Casino*, one of the mobsters met his demise (got whacked as they say) in a scene that depicted the alley at the back of the Steer. The secret door was a secret no more.

At the time, the maître d' would always be advised of the Founding Fathers' visit one hour in advance, and the menu was always the same and served family-style: Platters of antipasto, salamis, mortadella, capicola, pepperoncini, mushrooms, marinated red peppers, and artichoke hearts. Plates of buffalo mozzarella with beefsteak tomatoes and anchovies were also a must. Soup tureens with zuppa di pesce would follow. And then il secondo, the main course: Extra cut New York steaks (served rare) with pizzaiola sauce, veal saltimbocca, escarole with olive oil, garlic, and lemon, and mounds of rigatoni and penne with Bolognese and puttanesca sauces. Endless bottles of Barolo vino always flowed. Desserts were tiramisu and Cherries Jubilee flambé, while cigars and Sambuca capped the evening. Then the satiated guests disappeared through the secret door to their limousines, and away into the night they went.

In the once-upon-a-time tales of the Golden Steer Steakhouse, the restaurant occupied a space next to the Gold Rush Jewelry Store. One of the owners of that store was Anthony John Spilotro, an American mobster and enforcer for the Chicago Outfit in Las Vegas. In 1976, Spilotro opened the Gold Rush, a combination jewelry store and electronics factory. Here he fenced goods primarily obtained by his own burglary ring, which he formed with his brother Michael and Chicago bookmaker Herbert Blitzstein. The crew, led by feared hitman Frank Cullotta, became known as the Hole in the Wall Gang because of its penchant for gaining entry by drilling through the exterior walls and ceilings of the buildings they burglarized (also depicted in the movie *Casino*). Longtime Steer waiter Fabian remembers serving Mr. Spilotro and his entourage just three days before Spilotro and his brother were found dead, buried alive, in a cornfield in Enos, Indiana.

Yes, there are many colorful stories about the Golden Steer Steakhouse to regale curious listeners with. One relatively recent story worth sharing took place on October 9, 2008 when O. J. Simpson visited the Steer to have dinner with his lawyer and a couple of friends. Longtime Steer bartender Joe, who happens to be the godfather of O.J.'s daughter, Sydney Brooke, recalls O.J. ordering his usual prime rib, Diamond Jim cut (page 124). It was the night before O.J.'s sentencing for his part in an alleged robbery about a year prior at the Palace Station Hotel & Casino when O.J., along with five accomplices, went to retrieve the memorabilia O.J. claimed had been stolen from him. The evening before the jury delivered the verdict, O.J. dined at the Steer while laughing and announcing to Joe the bartender, "I'll be back here for dinner tomorrow night." That would not be the case. The following day, O.J. was found guilty of all of the charges against him. Judge Jackie Glass sentenced the "Juice" to thirty-three years, although the former NFL star served only nine years before the Nevada parole board decided to set him free.

The Steer Today

When the Golden Steer Steakhouse opened in 1958, the menu was very much the same as it is today, other than (needless to say) different prices. The once popular dinner special—soup and salad, fourteen-ounce New York steak with baked potato, vegetable du jour, and strawberry cheesecake for $6.75—is but a distant memory. The original menu, offered when the Steer first opened, remains on display in the memorabilia case in the lounge. There also wasn't any wine list to boast of, as there is today. In fact, original Steer owner Joe Kludjian admits he didn't serve any wine at all. "There wasn't any need for it," he recalls. "Martinis, Manhattans, bourbon, and scotch on the rocks were the call of the day." It wasn't until the early 1960s that Joe started to serve champagne, the popular beverage of choice for starlets from the lounges and hotel showrooms. When Joe eventually began to serve wine in the late '60s, there still wasn't a wine list. He simply offered the four "classic" wines of that time: Blue Nun Liebfraumilch, Lancers, and Mateus Rosé, along with Italian Chianti wrapped in a straw basket.

Today the Golden Steer's wine list has grown extensively, and you will find many of these world-class wines expertly paired with the wonderful food in this book for your edification. Proprietor Dr. Michael J. Signorelli is equally pleased with the culinary improvements the Steer has made over the years while never altering the menu or the restaurant aesthetics, both of which have made this time-tested restaurant so popular with locals and visitors of Las Vegas. As a former Rhode Islander landing in Las Vegas in 1969 by way of the US Air Force, Dr. Signorelli continues to reflect on how special it is to operate the Golden Steer in one of the most fascinating and exciting cities in the world. After stints as a real estate developer, hotel-casino owner, and Wall Street investor, Dr. Signorelli purchased the steak house in 2001. What he received was a five-star steakhouse, a historic landmark restaurant, an iconic establishment to share with family and friends, and a memorable venue that can never be duplicated. The Golden Steer Steakhouse remains decorated in American history while continuing to flourish, and it's doing so not through online advertising or social media, but via old-school word of mouth and a loyal following, which does come with a bit of irony. Dr. Signorelli's daughter, Amanda Signorelli, is

The Oldest Steakhouse in the City of Las Vegas
The Best Steaks On Earth
Est. 1958
Italian Specialties
Accompaniments
Fresh Broccoli
Creamed Spinach
Wild Rice
House Specialties
Sauces
Reserved

the CEO of Techweek, one of the nation's leading technology conferences for technology hubs around the country, according to *Inc. Magazine*. Despite her passion and in-depth knowledge for advanced technology, she agrees with her father that the Steer's success stems from staying true to what it is rather than trying to adapt or conform to today's ever-changing society, or to the throngs of millennials who visit Vegas every year. Dr. Signorelli, Johnny Burke, and the Golden Steer Steakhouse staff strongly believe that their restaurant, without making any further changes, will continue to thrive and prosper so long as there is a city called Las Vegas. Now, that's worth raising a glass and toasting to...

EXIT

SIGNATURE COCKTAILS

Golden Steer....25

Lemon Drop....26

Manhattan....29

Flamingo....32

Cosmopolitan....34

Moscow Mule....35

Dino's Long Pour Martini....36

GOLDEN STEER

Influenced by the French 75, the Golden Steer cocktail is the Golden Steer Steakhouse's own creation: a fun, light, and refreshing cognac-based drink suited for both the masculine and feminine palates. The blended ingredients take on a golden hue—perfect for the legendary steakhouse. Steer bartenders prefer to serve this cocktail in a tall champagne flute. While the coupe is fine for most drinks, every now and then you need a flute to lengthen the bubbles.

In a cocktail shaker filled with ice, add the cognac, lemon juice, and white peach puree. Shake well and strain into a chilled champagne flute. Top with champagne or Prosecco. Garnish and serve.

Serves 1

- 2 ounces Courvoisier cognac
- ½ lemon, juiced
- ½ ounce white peach puree
- Champagne or Prosecco
- Garnish: lemon twist and an Amarena cherry

LEMON DROP

Serves 1

- 3 ounces Ketel One Citroen vodka
- 2 ounces House-Made Sweet & Sour Mix (recipe follows)
- 2 ounces Cointreau or triple sec
- 1 dash lime juice
- 1 packet Sweet'N Low (or sugar)
- 1 lemon wedge
- Garnish: sugar rim and lemon wedge or wheel

A variation on the vodka martini, the Lemon Drop, presumably named after the lemon drop candy, is the invention of San Francisco bar owner Norman Jay Hobday, who introduced the drink in the 1970s. The lemony sweet-sour libation remains a requested cocktail at the Golden Steer. Managing partner John E. Burke says the secret to the Steer's Lemon Drop is in the House-Made Sweet & Sour Mix, made with lemonade, water, and sugar. The Steer also adds a packet of Sweet'N Low when preparing the drink, which some say is the real secret.

In a cocktail shaker filled with ice, add the vodka, House-Made Sweet & Sour Mix, Cointreau, lime juice, and Sweet'N Low. Squeeze the juice from the lemon wedge into the shaker then add the lemon wedge. Shake well and strain into a chilled martini glass rimmed with sugar. Garnish and serve.

HOUSE-MADE SWEET & SOUR MIX

Makes about 2 cups

- 1 cup unsweetened Minute Maid lemonade from concentrate
- 1 cup cold water
- ½ cup powdered sugar

In a suitable container, combine the unsweetened lemonade from concentrate, water, and powdered sugar. Mix well. Store in a sealed container in the refrigerator until ready to use, or up to 3 days.

MANHATTAN

Here's another delicious and oversized classic cocktail served at the Golden Steer Steakhouse. This drink originated on the East Coast in the late 1800s. The original called for American whiskey, sweet Italian vermouth, and Angostura bitters. During Prohibition, Canadian whiskey became a suitable replacement. Today Golden Steer Steakhouse bartenders stay true to the original recipe, opting for Maker's Mark, a Kentucky straight bourbon. They also add a kiss of cherry juice for sweetness.

In a cocktail shaker filled with ice, add the bourbon, sweet vermouth, bitters, and cherry juice. Shake well and strain into a chilled martini glass. Garnish and serve.

Serves 1 or 2

- 6 ounces Maker's Mark bourbon
- 1 ounce sweet Italian vermouth
- 1 dash aromatic bitters (preferably from Australian Bitters Company)
- 1 dash maraschino cherry juice
- Garnish: Amarena cherry

FLAMINGO

Serves 1 or 2

- 5 ounces Bacardi Dragon Berry rum
- ½ lime, juiced
- 1 dash Simple Syrup (recipe follows)
- 2 ounces House-Made Grenadine (recipe follows)
- Garnish: lime wedge or wheel

Another Golden Steer Steakhouse creation, this is a riff on the Pink Flamingo cocktail. Further influenced by the iconic Flamingo Las Vegas, which opened in 1946, and the Rat Pack (particularly Frank Sinatra, Dean Martin, and Sammy Davis Jr.) who played at the Flamingo and dined at the Steer, this sweet concoction is designed with the feminine palate in mind.

In a cocktail shaker filled with ice, add the rum, lime juice, Simple Syrup, and House-Made Grenadine. Shake well and strain into a chilled martini glass. Garnish and serve.

SIMPLE SYRUP

- 1 part cold water
- 1 part sugar

In a saucepot over medium-high heat, bring the water and sugar to a boil. Reduce the heat to low and stir constantly until the sugar dissolves completely and the mixture is clear, approximately 3 to 5 minutes. Remove from the heat and let cool. Refrigerate and store in a sealed container until ready to use.

HOUSE-MADE GRENADINE

- 1 part pomegranate juice
- 1 part powdered sugar

In a suitable container, combine the pomegranate juice and powdered sugar. Stir constantly until the sugar dissolves completely. Refrigerate and store in a sealed container until ready to use.

COSMOPOLITAN

Serves 1 or 2

- 4 ounces Ketel One Citroen vodka
- 2 ounces Cointreau or triple sec
- 1 dash Rose's Lime Juice (or ½ lime, juiced)
- 2 ounces cranberry juice
- Garnish: lime wedge or wheel, or lemon twist

Similar to the Lemon Drop, the Cosmopolitan is another iconic cocktail created in the 1970s and later introduced to the Golden Steer Steakhouse Signature Cocktails menu. Equally as popular, the Cosmo gained popularity in the late '90s and was further popularized among young women by television, particularly *Sex and the City*. For a good-tasting Cosmopolitan, it's important to use a lemon- or citrus-flavored vodka. The Steer prefers Ketel One Citroen. Due to the large number of Cosmos the steak house makes on any given night, bartenders often rely on a dash of Rose's Lime Juice, but you can use fresh lime juice when you're making this at home.

In a cocktail shaker filled with ice, add the vodka, Cointreau, Rose's Lime Juice, and cranberry juice. Shake well and strain into a chilled martini glass. Garnish and serve.

MOSCOW MULE

Although the Moscow Mule may seem relatively new to the bar scene, the cocktail has actually been around since 1941. Created by Connecticut spirit distributor John G. Martin, this mixed drink became an instant hit in Las Vegas in the 1940s, and was a favorite of casino owner William F. Harrah (of the famed Harrah's Hotel and Casinos). In keeping with tradition, the Golden Steer Steakhouse continues to serve up handcrafted Moscow Mules, which are best enjoyed in a copper mug. The Steer bartenders suggest using Barritt's Bermuda Stone Ginger Beer. This bold and zesty soft drink is bottled in Bermuda and dates back to the mid-1800s. (Note: To make a Kentucky Mule, simply replace the vodka with bourbon.)

Fill a copper mug with crushed ice. Add the vodka, lime juice, and Simple Syrup. Top with ginger beer. Garnish and serve.

Serves 1

- 2 ounces premium vodka (preferably Tito's Handmade Vodka)
- ½ lime, juiced
- 1 dash Simple Syrup (page 32)
- Ginger beer (preferably Barritt's)
- Garnish: fresh mint sprig

DINO'S LONG POUR MARTINI

Serves 1 or 2

- 6 ounces premium vodka or gin
- 1 ounce dry vermouth
- Garnish: 3 regular or blue-cheese-stuffed cocktail olives (optional)

This is the Golden Steer Steakhouse's version of the classic martini, arguably one of the most recognizable and coolest cocktails on the planet. Like all the Signature Cocktails in this chapter and served at the Steer, this martini is large, hence the name *Long Pour*. The drink conjures up images of tuxedos, beautiful women, and iconic celebrities. Sir Winston Churchill cherished the martini, as did Ernest Hemingway, Franklin Roosevelt, and Humphrey Bogart. Frequent Golden Steer Steakhouse patrons Dean Martin (after whom this cocktail is named) and Frank Sinatra were also fans of the martini, particularly Dean, who downed quite a few at the Steer during his tenure in Las Vegas.

In a cocktail shaker filled with ice, add the vodka or gin and dry vermouth. Shake well and strain into a chilled martini glass. Garnish and serve.

APPETIZERS

Oysters Rockefeller....42

Rhode Island Crab Cakes with Mayo-Mustard Sauce....44

Escargots de Bourgogne....46

Large Seafood-Stuffed Mushroom Caps....48

Toasted Ravioli with Marinara Sauce....53

Alaskan King Crab Cocktail....54

Jumbo Gulf Shrimp Cocktail....55

Narragansett Bay Clams Casino....56

Assorted Seafood Platter....60

Fresh Oysters on the Half Shell....62

Fried Calamari....63

OYSTERS ROCKEFELLER

This longtime and often-requested appetizer at the Golden Steer Steakhouse originated in New Orleans in 1899. Named after John D. Rockefeller, the richest American at the time, Oysters Rockefeller is a baked dish known for its fresh oysters and rich creamy sauce. The original recipe still remains a secret, but Golden Steer Steakhouse chefs incorporate one ingredient they believe is included in the original, and which they make in-house, Creamed Spinach. They also top off their Rockefeller with house-made Hollandaise Sauce.

Serves 1 or 2

- 6 fresh West Coast oysters
- 6 tablespoons Creamed Spinach (page 189)
- 6 dollops Hollandaise Sauce (page 200)
- Crumbled cooked bacon
- Butter lettuce, optional
- Lemon wedges

Preheat the oven to 350°F.

Shuck the oysters and arrange on a baking sheet. Top each oyster with 1 tablespoon of Creamed Spinach, 1 dollop of Hollandaise Sauce, and some crumbled bacon.

Place in the oven and bake for 8 to 10 minutes, or until slightly golden brown and bubbly.

Remove from the oven and arrange on a serving tray lined with butter lettuce, if desired. Serve with lemon wedges.

SUGGESTED PAIRING:

Clifford Bay Sauvignon Blanc, Marlborough, New Zealand

Sitting pretty on the northern tip of New Zealand's south island, Marlborough has become synonymous with New Zealand Sauvignon Blanc. As well it should be—Marlborough is the primary region for those delicious, citrusy, summer-lovin' wines with vibrant acidity and pungent, grassy, grapefruit flavors. This wine possesses a light straw color and tropical aromas of guava, melon, and citrus. The palate offers the same fine flavors followed by a crisp, dry, flinty finish.

RHODE ISLAND CRAB CAKES WITH MAYO-MUSTARD SAUCE

These crab cakes are an upscale, satisfying appetizer, and they're a taste of home to Golden Steer Steakhouse owner Dr. Michael J. Signorelli. If you live on the East Coast, you have a major source of food in your backyard. We're talking about blue crabs. These tasty crustaceans are available in good numbers in the summer months when the weather heats up. They're also fun to catch, and they're even more fun to eat. Blue crabs should be consumed soon after they're caught. They won't last very long in the refrigerator. Simply steam them for 8 to 10 minutes, then pick out the meat when they've cooled. For those on the West Coast, you can substitute the large sweet-tasting Dungeness crab for blue crabs. And if you don't have access to live-fresh crabs, you can often buy premium crabmeat already shelled at your local supermarket.

Makes about 9 (3-ounce) crab cakes

- 1 pound fresh blue crabmeat (or premium lump claw and crabmeat)
- 1 roasted red bell pepper, chopped (page 57)
- ¼ cup chopped green onions or scallions
- 1 egg
- 1 tablespoon Old Bay Seasoning
- ½ tablespoon ground mustard
- ½ lemon, juiced
- ½ tablespoon Worcestershire sauce
- 1 tablespoon fresh Italian parsley
- ½ cup mayonnaise
- ¾ cup bread crumbs, plus more for dusting and sprinkling on the cookie sheet
- 2 tablespoons olive oil
- Flour, for dusting
- Fresh Italian parsley, for garnish
- Lemon wedges, for garnish
- Cocktail Sauce (page 54)
- Mayo-Mustard Sauce (recipe follows)

In a mixing bowl, combine the crabmeat, red bell pepper, green onions, egg, Old Bay Seasoning, ground mustard, lemon juice, Worcestershire, parsley, mayonnaise, and bread crumbs. Mix well to combine.

With wet hands, scoop up about 3 ounces of the crab mixture and form into a 1-inch-thick cake. Set aside and repeat with the remaining mixture until about nine cakes are formed. Next, dust each cake in the bread crumbs, shaking off the excess, and arrange on a cookie sheet layered with a dusting of bread crumbs so the cakes don't stick. Refrigerate for at least 1 hour for the cakes to bind.

Preheat the oven to 350°F.

In a large sauté pan, heat the olive oil over medium heat.

Remove the crab cakes from refrigerator and dust in flour, shaking off the excess. Add the crab cakes to the pan, being careful not to overcrowd it; work in batches. Cook the cakes until golden brown and turn them over. Remove from the heat and place in the oven. Bake for about 4 minutes, then flip again and bake for an additional 3 or 4 minutes until both sides are brown and crispy. Remove from the oven, garnish with parsley, and serve with lemon wedges and a side of Cocktail Sauce and Mayo-Mustard Sauce.

MAYO-MUSTARD SAUCE

Makes about 1 cup

- 1 cup mayonnaise
- ½ lemon, juiced
- 2–3 dashes Tabasco hot sauce
- 1 pinch chopped fresh Italian parsley
- 1 teaspoon Worcestershire sauce
- 1 pinch white pepper
- 1 teaspoon ground mustard
- 1 teaspoon red wine vinegar

In a mixing bowl, combine the mayonnaise, lemon juice, Tabasco, parsley, Worcestershire, pepper, mustard, and vinegar. Whisk until smooth and creamy. Refrigerate until ready to use.

SUGGESTED PAIRING:

Santa Margherita Pinot Grigio, Alto Adige, Italy

The northernmost region of Italy is fairly hilly due to its closeness to the Alps, and many vines in Trentino are terraced along the hillsides for ideal sunlight benefits. Alto Adige, in turn, has more vines on the valley floors but enjoys warmer summers. Straw yellow in color, this wine has a crisp fragrance followed by fresh, harmonious fruit set off by slight sweetness and a long finish full of delicate, tangy flavor.

ESCARGOTS DE BOURGOGNE

Considered the house specialty at the Golden Steer Steakhouse, this classic appetizer originated in the French region of Burgundy. The Steer prepares the dish using large, tender snails from Indonesia, which are carefully cleaned, cooked, and packed in water, salt, and spices. Although the steakhouse elects to serve escargots in elegant snail plates, you can also serve them in their shells or in mushroom caps for added attraction. Be sure to rinse the snails before serving. You can also simmer them in white wine to enhance their flavor.

Serves 2

- 2 tablespoons Lemon-Garlic Butter (recipe follows)
- 12 large, tender snails
- Bread crumbs
- Lemon wedges

Preheat the oven to 350°F.

In a small ovenproof sauté pan, add the butter, and place over medium heat. When the butter is melted, add the snails. Sauté for about 3 minutes. Remove from the heat and sprinkle the bread crumbs over the top. Place the pan in the oven for 8 to 10 minutes. Remove and transfer to a serving dish, along with the lemon wedges.

LEMON-GARLIC BUTTER

Makes about 1 cup

- 1 cup salted butter, softened to room temperature
- 2 teaspoons minced garlic
- ½ teaspoon Worcestershire sauce
- 1 teaspoon chopped fresh Italian parsley
- 3 tablespoons white wine

In a mixing bowl, add the butter, garlic, Worcestershire, parsley, and white wine. Whisk until well combined. Refrigerate the unused portion for up to 1 week.

SUGGESTED PAIRING:

Old World Chardonnay, Drouhin-Vaudon Chablis Premier Cru, Burgundy, France

Joseph Drouhin owns around fifteen acres of vines in the Valley of Vauvillien, nestled between the Mont de Milieu and Monte de Tonnerre Premier Cru vineyards. The name Moulin de Vaudon comes from the watermill nearby, owned by the Drouhin family and straddling the Serein River. This dry unoaked wine is typical of Chablis with a brilliant yellow color, aromas of citrus, and a nice texture on the palate with fruity and mineral flavors.

LARGE SEAFOOD-STUFFED MUSHROOM CAPS

These mushrooms, stuffed with shrimp, crab, scallops, and herbs, make a delicious—and easy—bite of Golden Steer Steakhouse–inspired flavors that complement any meal or gathering. While Steer chefs make these fresh daily, you can stuff, cover, and store your stuffed mushrooms up to a day in advance for a make-ahead appetizer that's sure to please. Remember to select the freshest seafood available as well as hand-selecting the mushrooms, which should be large, firm, evenly colored, and uniform in shape with no broken or discolored caps. The caps should also be tightly closed. If all the gills are showing, the mushrooms are past their prime. Cultivated white mushrooms are the preferred mushroom served at the Golden Steer Steakhouse because of their mild, earthy flavor and their year-round availability. For home cooks, try the clam base from Better Than Bouillon (also available at most markets and online), made from select cooked clams and spices.

Makes about 24 (6 per serving)

- 2 cups heavy cream
- 2 large fresh wild-caught shrimp, peeled, de-veined, and finely chopped
- 1 cup fresh crabmeat (or premium lump claw and crabmeat)
- 1 cup fresh bay scallops, finely chopped
- ½ shallot, peeled and diced
- 1 large pinch white pepper
- 1 large pinch whole dried (or fresh) thyme
- 5 tablespoons salted butter, divided
- ¼ cup white wine
- 1 teaspoon concentrated clam base
- ¼ cup flour
- 24 fresh large cultivated white mushrooms, washed (never soaked)
- Paprika, as needed
- Chicken stock, as needed
- Lemon wedges, for garnish

In a sauté pan over medium heat, add the cream, shrimp, crab, scallops, shallot, pepper, thyme, 1 tablespoon of the butter, and the white wine. Stir well to combine, and cook for about 2 minutes. Stir in the clam base and reduce the heat, allowing the mixture to simmer for about 4 or 5 minutes, reducing the cream.

In separate sauté pan, whisk the flour and remaining ¼ cup of butter over medium-low heat until a roux is formed. This is the thickening agent for the seafood mixture. Add 1 tablespoon of roux at a time to the seafood mixture while it continues to cook, until the mixture achieves the consistency of oatmeal. Remove from the heat and let cool.

Preheat the oven to 350°F.

Remove the stems from the mushroom and invert. Fill each mushroom cap with some of the cooled seafood mixture. Sprinkle the tops with a little paprika and arrange in an ovenproof casserole dish. Fill the bottom of the dish with a thin layer of chicken stock. Place in the oven and bake for 10 minutes, or until toasted and golden brown. Remove from the oven and serve with lemon wedges.

SUGGESTED PAIRING:

Santa Margherita Prosecco Superiore, Italy

Nestled in the hills of the eastern Veneto is one of the world's most wonderful wine-growing regions. In April 2010, this small area was established as a DOCG region, the highest quality designation that can be given to an Italian wine. Glera grapes are grown on the steep hillsides and 100 percent hand-harvested. Straw yellow in color, this wine exhibits a fine fruity fragrance, an elegant long-lived mousse, and a pleasantly dry well-balanced acidity on the palate.

TOASTED RAVIOLI WITH MARINARA SAUCE

Arguably one of the most popular appetizers on the Golden Steer Steakhouse menu, Toasted Ravioli contain the perfect crunch to accompany the explosion of flavor packed inside. Originating from the Italian neighborhood of St. Louis, Missouri, known as The Hill, these lightly breaded deep-fried ravioli, which are served with a side of house-made Marinara Sauce for dipping, are a must-have when dining at the Steer or entertaining at home. Golden Steer chefs prefer ravioli stuffed with either provolone or Parmesan cheese (traditional New England) as opposed to beef, veal, or chicken (common stuffings in St. Louis and the Midwest).

Makes about a dozen (8 per serving)

- 3 eggs
- ½ cup milk
- Flour, for dusting
- Bread crumbs, for dusting
- 12 fresh cheese ravioli
- Vegetable oil, as needed, for deep-frying
- Chopped fresh Italian parsley, for garnish
- Fresh-grated Parmesan cheese, for garnish
- Marinara Sauce (page 157)

In a mixing bowl, whisk the eggs and milk until well combined.

Place the flour and bread crumbs in two separate bowls.

Prepare the ravioli in batches by first dusting them in the flour, shaking off the excess. Then add the ravioli to the egg-milk mixture and coat well. Finally, toss the ravioli in the bread crumbs, shaking off the excess. When you're ready to cook, carefully add the ravioli to the hot oil and deep-fry until golden brown, about 1 or 2 minutes. Remove from the oil and drain on paper towels. Top with the parsley and Parmesan, and serve with a side of the house-made Marinara Sauce.

SUGGESTED PAIRING:

Trumer Pils Beer, Berkeley, California

All the ingredients used in this beer are "traditional" (shipped from Austria) with the exception of the water, which is from the High Sierras. Hops used in the recipe include Czech Saaz, German Hallertau Perle, and Spalt Select. Trumer is further aged six weeks prior to bottling. A German-style Pilsner, Trumer Pils is characterized by a distinct hops flavor, high carbonation, and light body. The combination of hops, the malt mashing process, and a proprietary yeast make Trumer Pils unique among beers.

ALASKAN KING CRAB COCKTAIL

Serves 2

- 2 Alaskan king crab legs
- 2 leaves butter lettuce
- Fresh Italian parsley, for garnish
- Lemon wedges, for serving
- Cocktail Sauce (recipe follows)
- Tabasco hot sauce (optional)

This cocktail showcases the succulent sweet meat from the largest crab in US waters—the red king crab. Plucked from the icy depths of Alaska's Bering Sea, king crab are delivered live to the docks, just as we've seen on the television series *Deadliest Catch*. However, almost all of the catch is cleaned, cooked, and frozen before being shipped to markets around the country as either sections (legs and thorax) or separate legs and claws. When the massive king crab legs arrive at the Golden Steer Steakhouse, chefs defrost them and remove the succulent meat, which takes center stage in this mouthwatering appetizer.

Defrost the king crab legs and remove the meat; set aside.

Fill a vintage shrimp cocktail glass bowl (or martini glass) with crushed ice (fill a martini glass three-quarters of the way). Place a lettuce leaf inside the bowl, or on top of the ice if you're using a martini glass. Arrange the crabmeat in a large mound on top of the lettuce leaf. Garnish with parsley, and serve with lemon wedges and a side of Cocktail Sauce and Tabasco, if desired.

COCKTAIL SAUCE

Makes about 1 cup

- 1 cup California sweet chili sauce (Heinz)
- ¾ tablespoon horseradish sauce
- ½ lemon, juiced
- 2–3 dashes Worcestershire sauce

In a small bowl, combine the chili sauce, horseradish sauce, lemon juice, and Worcestershire. Mix well and refrigerate until ready to serve. This sauce will keep for up to 2 weeks.

SUGGESTED PAIRING:

G. H. Mumm, Cordon Rouge Champagne

Georges Hermann Mumm is the man to thank for the Golden Steer Steakhouse's iconic cuvée. In 1876, to assert the quality of its champagne, Mumm decided to adorn its bottles with a red silk ribbon, a reference to the Ordre de Saint-Louis and the Grand Cordon de la Légion d'Honneur. This particular champagne reveals initial aromas of ripe fresh fruit (white and yellow peaches, apricots) and tropical notes (lychee and pineapple), then opens up with the fragrance of vanilla before developing notes of milky caramel, bread crumbs, and yeast, culminating in aromas of dried fruit and honey.

JUMBO GULF SHRIMP COCKTAIL

Like the Alaskan King Crab Cocktail, this classic appetizer is about the large grade-A wild-caught shrimp from the United States, close to the Gulf of Mexico. Gulf shrimp are tastier, more tender, and, most important, fresher than those foreign—and not so sustainable—imports. Because Gulf shrimp are what they call free swimmers, their texture is usually firmer than pond-raised shrimp. They are also high in protein with little to no fat or carbohydrates. Golden Steer Steakhouse chefs prefer using the white Gulf shrimp as opposed to the brown or pink varieties because white shrimp have a sweeter flavor with a firm, slightly "crunchy" texture. This appetizer happens to be a favorite of loyal Golden Steer Steakhouse patron Mario Andretti, world champion race car driver and one of the most successful Americans in the history of the sport.

Serves 2

- 1 tablespoon McCormick Pickling Spice
- 1 lemon, cut into wedges
- 8 large wild-caught white jumbo Gulf shrimp
- Fresh Italian parsley, for garnish
- Cocktail Sauce (page 54)
- Tabasco hot sauce (optional)

In a pot of water, add the pickling spice and the juice squeezed from two of the lemon wedges. Place over high heat and bring to a boil. Add the shrimp and cook through, about 5 minutes. Remove the shrimp and let cool. Remove the head and shell, but keep the tail intact. De-vein the shrimp and refrigerate until ready to serve.

Fill vintage shrimp cocktail glass bowls (or martini glasses) with crushed ice. Arrange four shrimp on the edge of each serving vessel. Garnish with parsley, and serve with lemon wedges, and a side of Cocktail Sauce and Tabasco, if desired.

SUGGESTED PAIRING:

Bellavista Franciacorta

This is a sparkling wine made in Franciacorta in Lombardia, Italy, using the same methods as champagne. Combining elegance and depth, it tastes of sweet ripe fruit, meringue, and pastries; it's creamy on the palate. A distinguishing factor that adds value and uniqueness to this Gran Cuvée is the fermentation and production of at least 35 percent of its wines in small white oak barrels that are more than thirty-five years old.

NARRAGANSETT BAY CLAMS CASINO

Serves 1 or 2

- 5 large fresh clams
- Clam Mixture (recipe follows)
- Crumbled cooked bacon
- Lettuce, for garnish, if desired
- Lemon wedges, for garnish

Like Rhode Island Crab Cakes, this appetizer originates from Golden Steer Steakhouse owner Dr. Michael J. Signorelli's home state of Rhode Island. Since its introduction in 1917, Clams Casino has remained a popular American classic, particularly with Italian Americans. It was also the requested appetizer by regular Steer guest Frank Sinatra, who'd eat dozens at a time before moving on to his main course (see Frank's Menu, page 104). When making this savory appetizer at home, after you shuck the clams and pack them with the Clam Mixture, you can stop and freeze the clams for up to 1 week if you prefer to serve them later. To prepare, simply defrost for 2 minutes in the microwave (do not cook) and finish in the oven as noted below.

Preheat the oven to 350°F.

Shuck each clam to loosen the clam meat from the muscle. Keep the meat in the shell, and detach and discard the other/empty shell. Next, pack the clamshell with 1 or 2 tablespoons of Clam Mixture, depending on its size. The mixture should be rounded off on top. Add some crumbled bacon to the top of the mixture, pressing slightly so the bacon doesn't fall off. Arrange the clams on a baking sheet.

Place the sheet of clams in the oven and bake for 8 to 10 minutes, or until golden brown.

Remove from the oven and arrange the baked clams on a serving tray lined with lettuce (if desired) and accompanied by lemon wedges.

CLAM MIXTURE

Makes enough mixture for 12 clams

- ½ roasted red bell pepper, diced
- 2 tablespoons olive oil
- ¼ yellow onion, peeled and diced
- ½ teaspoon minced garlic
- 2 pinches dried oregano
- 2 pinches white pepper
- 1 pinch salt
- 1 tablespoon salted butter
- ¼ cup white wine
- 1 cup chopped clams
- ½ cup clam juice
- ½ cup bread crumbs

Roast a red bell pepper by placing it under the broiler or on a hot outdoor barbecue, turning often to blister all sides. When the skin is charred and soft, remove from the heat and immediately place in a paper bag, foil, or sealed container to trap the steam. Keep sealed for about 10 minutes. Slice the roasted pepper, removing the stem, seeds, and loose skin, and dice.

Heat the olive oil in a sauté pan over medium heat. When it's hot, add the diced pepper, onion, garlic, oregano, pepper, salt, and butter. Let it cook for about 2 minutes. Add the white wine and reduce the heat to low, letting the mixture simmer for about 3 minutes. Add the chopped clams and clam juice, and simmer for another 3 to 4 minutes. Stir in the bread crumbs to thicken the mixture. Remove from the heat and let cool.

SUGGESTED PAIRING:

Clarksburg Wine Company Chenin Blanc,
Clarksburg, California

The Clarksburg region is known for growing arguably the best Chenin Blanc, Petite Sirah, and Cabernet Franc grapes in all of California. This wine presents an inviting nose packed with sweet fruit and intriguing floral notes. Initial hints of musky melon and juicy pear intermingle with a floral character that resembles apple blossom. The wine's racy acidity perfectly frames the stone-fruit-driven flavor and luxurious mouthfeel. The finish is long with notes of citrus pith and minerality.

ASSORTED SEAFOOD PLATTER

This colossal appetizer is an elegant starter for two or more who crave fresh, mouthwatering seafood. At the Golden Steer Steakhouse, an assortment of fresh oysters, Gulf shrimp, Alaskan king crab, and a lobster tail is served on a bed of crushed ice accompanied by lemon wedges, Tabasco, and house-made Cocktail Sauce and horseradish sauce. While we've discussed previously in this chapter the kind of oysters, Gulf shrimp, and Alaskan king crab served at the Golden Steer, we should mention the particular lobster preferred for this beautiful dish: live Maine (American) lobster. These are the lobsters of choice because they have two large claws, which are added to the platter to accompany the tail. When you're making your selections at the seafood counter, ask enough questions to be sure what you're buying is, in fact, a Maine lobster and not one from another state or Canada.

Serves 2

- 6 Fresh Oysters on the Half Shell (page 62)
- 6 cooked large wild-caught white jumbo Gulf shrimp (page 55)
- 1 large Alaskan king crab leg (page 141), cut into sections
- 1 cooked Australian lobster tail (page 140), but one can also use Maine lobster
- Lemon wedges, for garnish
- Cocktail Sauce (page 54)
- Horseradish sauce
- Tabasco hot sauce

Fill a large, deep platter or bowl with crushed ice. Arrange the oysters around the edge of one side, and the shrimp on the opposite side. Place the crab and lobster sections in the center of the platter, and garnish with lemon wedges. Serve with a side of Cocktail Sauce, horseradish sauce, and Tabasco.

SUGGESTED PAIRING:

Perrier-Jouët Belle Epoque Champagne, Reims, France

Perrier-Jouët was founded in 1811 in Epernay by Pierre-Nicolas-Marie Perrier and his wife, Adele Jouët. One of the most prestigious houses in Champagne, the firm was shipping wine to Great Britain by 1813 and to the United States by 1837. This particular champagne exhibits the lightness of white floral notes: hawthorn blossom, linden blossom, and white clover. A fresh, stylish champagne with good structure, silky and elegant, this varietal is based on the mineral notes of the best Chardonnay Grand Crus. The floral, fruity notes give way to subtle spicy hints for a pleasant finish on the palate.

Reserved

FRESH OYSTERS ON THE HALF SHELL

Serves 1 or 2

- 6 fresh West Coast oysters
- Fresh Italian parsley, for garnish
- Lemon wedges
- Cocktail Sauce (page 54)
- Horseradish sauce
- Tabasco hot sauce (optional)

Freshness is a common and important element at the Golden Steer Steakhouse, particularly when it comes to seafood, like these fresh oysters. Chefs at the Steer prefer West Coast oysters, which have a creamy white flesh. In today's market, more and more oysters are being grown by aquaculturists on strings or nets, relieving the press on wild oyster populations. Companies like Penn Cove Shellfish in Washington State, which delivers fresh oysters to the Steer on a weekly basis, strive to provide the finest in sustainable and delicious farmed shellfish. Oysters, incidentally, get their specific tastes from the areas where they are grown, and they are often sold under these place-names.

Layer a suitable serving tray with crushed ice. Shuck the oysters and arrange on the ice. Garnish with parsley, and serve with lemon wedges and a side of Cocktail Sauce, horseradish, and Tabasco, if desired.

SUGGESTED PAIRING:

Dino's Long Pour Martini (page 36)

FRIED CALAMARI

Another appetizer often requested at the Golden Steer Steakhouse is Fried Calamari, which is made using fresh market squid from the near-shore waters off California. Compared with other squid, market squid are relatively small, averaging seven to twelve inches in length, making them the perfect size for calamari rings. Because of the increased awareness of the health benefits of eating seafood, US consumption of market squid is on the rise. Whenever possible, purchase fresh, cleaned squid rather than frozen. Although the Golden Steer Steakhouse serves only rings in its Fried Calamari, feel free to fry the tentacles, too. Fresh, cooked squid, like in this delicious appetizer, should taste mild, sweet, and tender with the perfect crunch.

Serves 1 or 2

- 3 eggs
- ½ cup milk
- 3 cups bread crumbs
- 1 cup flour
- 2 tablespoons Seasoned salt (preferably Lawry's)
- Vegetable oil, as needed, for deep-frying
- 7 ounces fresh squid tubes, sliced into 1-inch rings (and tentacles, if desired)
- Chopped fresh Italian parsley, for garnish
- Lemon wedges, for garnish
- Marinara Sauce (page 157) or Tartar Sauce (recipe follows)

In a mixing bowl, whisk the eggs and milk until well combined.

In a separate bowl, combine the bread crumbs, flour, and seasoned salt.

Heat a deep fryer or deep pot or wok with vegetable oil until hot.

Add the squid to the egg-milk mixture and coat well. Then toss the squid in the bread crumb mixture, shaking off the excess. Carefully add the squid to the hot oil and deep-fry until golden brown, about 1 or 2 minutes. Remove from the oil and drain on paper towels. Top with chopped parsley and serve with lemon wedges and a side of Marinara Sauce or Tartar Sauce.

TARTAR SAUCE

Makes about 1½ cups

- 1 tablespoon chopped yellow onion
- 1 tablespoon chopped parsley
- 1 pinch white pepper
- 1 teaspoon Worcestershire sauce
- ½ lemon, juiced
- 1 teaspoon Dijon mustard
- 1½ cups mayonnaise

In a mixing bowl, combine the onion, parsley, pepper, Worcestershire, lemon juice, mustard, and mayonnaise. Whisk until smooth and creamy. Refrigerate until ready to use.

SUGGESTED PAIRING:

New Belgium Snapshot Wheat Beer

When some souring bacteria is added to a portion of this beer's overall wort, a lactic acid is produced that gives the beer a unique sourness and mouthfeel. This acidic portion is then added to another portion of the wort, which is fermented along with the ale yeast. The result is two worts—a sour and a regular—that are blended together to make Snapshot. This beer is lively, refreshing, and balanced, with a nice tart zing. Snapshot is flavorful and doesn't sacrifice anything. While this beer is intended for mainstream audiences as an introductory sour, beer geeks will be just as happy adding it to a drinking mix.

STOCKS, ROUX & SOUPS

House-Made Beef Stock (Au Jus)....68

House-Made Chicken Stock....69

Chicken & Rice....71

Chicken Noodle....72

Roux....73

Beef Barley....75

French Onion....76

Manhattan Clam Chowder....79

HOUSE-MADE BEEF STOCK *(AU JUS)*

Makes about 5 cups

- 2 cups scrap beef and beef bones
- 1 large carrot, peeled and finely chopped
- 1 large celery stalk, finely chopped
- ½ yellow onion, peeled and finely chopped
- 5 cups cold water
- 1 teaspoon browning and seasoning sauce
- 2 teaspoons concentrated beef base

At the Golden Steer Steakhouse, this homemade stock is made daily and used in a number of dishes, including French Onion Soup, Veal Marsala, Peppercorn Sauce, as a finishing drizzle on hand-cut steaks, and as the *Au Jus* accompanying Prime Rib. This particular beef stock is rich in flavor because Steer chefs incorporate natural beef trimmings and bones with a browning and seasoning sauce (a vegetable base available at most markets and online), and a concentrated beef base. For home cooks, try the beef base from Better Than Bouillon (also available at most markets and online), made from roast beef and concentrated beef stock.

In a stockpot over medium heat, add the beef and bones, carrots, celery, onion, cold water, browning and seasoning sauce, and beef base. Bring to a boil, then reduce the heat to a simmer. Cover the pot and let the stock cook for 10 to 15 minutes. Remove from the heat and strain into another stockpot. Keep warm until ready to use.

HOUSE-MADE CHICKEN STOCK

Like the House-Made Beef Stock, this chicken stock is also made daily at the Golden Steer Steakhouse and used in a number of dishes. It's the base for Chicken & Rice and Chicken Noodle Soups, and it's used in the Sautéed Mushrooms. Steer chefs also incorporate the stock into many of their seafood dishes, as well as the Fresh Brook Trout and Frog Legs on the Vintage Selections menu. For home cooks, try the chicken base from Better Than Bouillon (available at most markets and online), made from chicken meat and natural chicken juices, for a rich chicken-flavored stock.

Makes 3 or 4 quarts

- 1 whole chicken
- 1 large carrot, peeled and finely chopped
- 1 large celery stalk, finely chopped
- ½ yellow onion, peeled and finely chopped
- ¼ cup chicken base, more or less to taste

Add the chicken to a large stockpot. Fill the pot three-quarters of the way full with cold water, covering the chicken. Place over medium-high heat. Add the carrot, celery, onion, and chicken base; bring to a boil. Reduce the heat to a simmer, cover, and cook—stirring occasionally—until the chicken is cooked through and falls off the bone, about 30 minutes.

When the chicken is fully cooked, remove the pot from the heat and take the chicken meat out of the pot. Note: you can either discard the chicken or reserve the meat for another use like making Chicken & Rice (page 71) or Chicken Noodle (page 72) soup. Strain the liquid into another stockpot. Keep warm until ready to use.

CHICKEN & RICE

Every soup at the Golden Steer Steakhouse is made from scratch. This classic chicken soup is also good for you and serves as a source of essential nutrients, which is why many people rely on chicken soup when they're feeling under the weather. Just be sure you're making one of the Golden Steer Steakhouse chicken soups and not reaching for a can, as the canned varieties often come loaded with sodium, reducing their nutritional value. For a healthier soup, use a low- or no-sodium chicken base.

Serves 6

- 1 whole chicken
- 1 large carrot, peeled and finely chopped
- 1 large celery stalk, finely chopped
- ½ yellow onion, peeled and finely chopped
- ¼ cup chicken base, more or less to taste
- 6 cups wild rice
- Chopped fresh Italian parsley, for garnish

Add the chicken to a large stockpot. Fill the pot three-quarters of the way full with cold water, covering the chicken. Place over medium-high heat. Add the carrot, celery, onion, and chicken base; bring to a boil. Reduce the heat to a simmer, cover, and cook—stirring occasionally—until the chicken is cooked through and falling off the bone, about 30 minutes.

Meanwhile, cook the wild rice by simply boiling it in unsalted water until it's tender.

When the chicken is fully cooked, remove the pot from the heat. Take the chicken out of the pot and let it cool. When it's cool to the touch, remove the meat from the carcass, chop it, and return the meat to the pot.

Drain the cooked rice and add to the pot.

To serve, ladle the Chicken & Rice Soup into individual serving bowls. Garnish with some chopped parsley and serve.

SUGGESTED PAIRING:

Hahn GSM (Grenache, Syrah, Mourvedre), Central Coast, California

Nicky Hahn grew up speaking German. In his native language, the word Hahn means "rooster," which is why a depiction of this bird has always graced the label of Hahn wines. From the beginning, Nicky strove to produce exceptional varietal wines from Monterey County where the Hahn Family Wines vineyards and winery are located. Each of the three grape types blended into this wine adds distinctive aromas and flavors. Grenache contributes raspberry, strawberry, and cherry flavors, while Syrah lends color, tannins, and hints of blueberry and black pepper. The Mourvedre adds richness to the mid-palate and lengthens the dry finish.

CHICKEN NOODLE

In the United States and Canada, it's common to have noodles in your chicken soup. The Golden Steer Steakhouse relies on using fresh, premium chicken as opposed to the time when American chicken soup was prepared using old hens too tough and stringy to be roasted or cooked. These days, young broiler chickens have replaced old chickens on the market. As with the previous recipe, use a low- or no-sodium chicken base for a healthier soup.

Serves 6

- 1 whole chicken
- 1 large carrot, peeled and finely chopped
- 1 large celery stalk, finely chopped
- ½ yellow onion, peeled and finely chopped
- ¼ cup chicken base, more or less to taste
- 6 cups pasta noodles (if using spaghetti, break noodles into small pieces)
- Chopped fresh Italian parsley, for garnish

Add the chicken to a large stockpot. Fill the pot three-quarters of the way full with cold water, covering the chicken. Place over medium-high heat. Add the carrots, celery, onions, and chicken base; bring to a boil. Reduce the heat to a simmer, cover, and cook—stirring occasionally—until the chicken is cooked through and falling off bone, about 30 minutes.

Meanwhile, cook the pasta by simply boiling it in unsalted water until it's al dente.

When the chicken is fully cooked, remove the pot from the heat. Take the chicken out of the pot and let it cool. When it's cool to the touch, remove the meat from the carcass and chop. Return the meat to the pot.

Drain the cooked pasta and add it to the pot.

To serve, ladle the Chicken Noodle Soup into individual serving bowls. Garnish with some chopped parsley and serve.

SUGGESTED PAIRING:

Hahn GSM (Grenache, Syrah, Mourvedre), Central Coast, California

Georges Duboeuf Fleurie, Beaujolais, France

Fleurie is a terroir that sits on hillsides of beautiful pink granite covered in climbing Gamay grapes. These vines work their roots into the rocks to draw their substance and infuse Fleurie wine with the scent and spirit of the elegant region. Elegant and fine, Fleurie has an intense crimson color and reveals a range of fruity and floral aromas: iris, violets, roses, red berries, and wild peaches.

ROUX

Yes, it's only two ingredients, but Golden Steer Steakhouse chefs depend on this simple light-colored ("white") roux in the kitchen, and so should you. The purpose of roux is to act as a thickening agent in various sauces you'll see in this book. These include the creamier seafood and vegetable sauces, as well as steak sauces like Pizzaiola, which Frank Sinatra insisted he have atop his New York strip steak before performing.

- 1 part olive oil
- 1 part flour

In a sauté pan or stockpot over low heat, combine 1 part olive oil with 1 part flour; mix well. Cook the Roux, stirring frequently, until it reaches the consistency of a smooth paste. Remove from the heat and reserve until ready to use.

BEEF BARLEY

Living in the twenty-first century doesn't mean you can't make a soup from the eighteenth century. This particular soup crafted by the Golden Steer Steakhouse chefs is a take on the original, which called for turnips, mutton, and ham. It's also great to see barley in a soup, which is often overlooked these days when rice, corn, and wheat are so predominant. Even though the Golden Steer includes cuts of prime New York strip and filet mignon in its Beef Barley, you can use a less expensive cut of beef, such as top sirloin, when making this soup at home.

Serves 4

- 5 cups cold water
- 2 cups barley, soaked in water overnight and drained
- 1 large carrot, peeled and finely chopped
- 1 large celery stalk, finely chopped
- ½ yellow onion, peeled and finely chopped
- 1 cup tomato puree
- ½ teaspoon minced garlic
- 1 pinch white pepper
- 1½ tablespoons chicken base, more or less to taste
- 2 cups uncooked cubed beef (preferably New York strip or filet mignon)
- Chopped fresh Italian parsley, for garnish

In a stockpot over medium-high heat, combine the water, barley, carrot, celery, onion, tomato puree, garlic, white pepper, chicken base, and cubed beef. Bring to a boil, reduce the heat to low, cover, and let simmer for 20 to 30 minutes.

To serve, ladle the Beef Barley Soup into individual serving bowls. Garnish with some chopped parsley and serve.

SUGGESTED PAIRING:

Trapiche Broquel Malbec, Mendoza, Argentina

Trapiche is located in the province of Mendoza, Argentina, with the winery inspired by the Italian Renaissance. Biodynamics and ecological agricultural practices respect that the moon cycles and the position of other planets influence the vines. Purple-red in color with ruby highlights, this Malbec exudes aromas of fresh red and black fruits, floral notes, earthy minerals, and a touch of smoke. It's rich and spicy on the palate with a long pleasant finish.

FRENCH ONION

Onion soup has been enjoyed as far back as Roman times. It was also a soup reserved for poor people because onions were so abundant and easy to grow. At the turn of the eighteenth century, France upped onion soup quality by adding beef stock and caramelized onions. By 1960, about the time the Golden Steer Steakhouse first opened its doors, this soup had become popular on American menus. Although there are many different recipes for it today, the Steer's French Onion Soup is a rich and simple rendition of the French classic.

Serves 4

- 1 tablespoon olive oil
- 1 yellow onion, peeled and thinly sliced
- ½ teaspoon minced garlic
- 1 pinch white pepper
- 3 bay leaves
- 6 cups House-Made Beef Stock (page 68)
- 1 tablespoon beef base
- 1 tablespoon white wine
- 4 slices French baguette
- 12 slices Swiss cheese
- Fresh-grated Parmesan cheese, as needed
- Paprika, as needed

Heat the olive oil in a stockpot over medium-low heat. Add the onion, garlic, pepper, and bay leaves. Cook, stirring often, until the onion is soft, about 5 minutes. Add the House-Made Beef Stock, beef base, and white wine. Reduce the heat to low, cover, and let simmer for 10 to 15 minutes.

Preheat the oven to broil.

Ladle the soup into French onion soup bowls or other similar-sized ovenproof bowls, discarding the bay leaves. Top with a slice of French baguette, 3 slices of Swiss cheese, and a pinch of Parmesan and paprika. Place under the broiler until the cheese is melted and golden brown. Remove from the oven and serve.

SUGGESTED PAIRING:

Marc Brédif Vouvray Chenin Blanc,
Loire, France

Marc Brédif wines are made in a state-of-the art winery within the landmark Château du Nozet, and are considered to be some of the finest examples grown on the lower slopes along the Loire Valley. The vineyards have soils of mainly chalk clay, and the vineyards are twenty-five to thirty years old on average. This particular wine is a medium-dry white wine with balanced acidity, as well as delicate overtones of wood and honeysuckle. Wonderful smells of white fruit are followed by pear and fig flavors with a toasted hazelnut finish.

MANHATTAN CLAM CHOWDER

In homage to the Portuguese immigrants from Rhode Island who were the first to add tomatoes to their chowder, Golden Steer Steakhouse owner Dr. Michael J. Signorelli, who hails from Rhode Island, prefers the lighter Manhattan variety of clam chowder as opposed to the thicker New England clam chowder made with milk or cream. For home cooks, try to use fresh clams and clam juice whenever possible. Also use a quality clam base, such as Better Than Bouillon (available at most markets and online), made from select cooked clams and spices.

Serves 6

- 1 tablespoon olive oil
- 1 large carrot, peeled and finely chopped
- 1 large celery stalk, finely chopped
- ½ yellow onion, peeled and finely chopped
- 2 bay leaves
- 1 teaspoon minced garlic
- 1 pinch white pepper
- 5 cups cold water
- 1 cup tomato puree
- ¼ potato, peeled, cooked, and small cubed
- 1½ cups chopped clams
- ½ cup clam juice
- 1 teaspoon clam base
- Fresh Italian parsley, for garnish

Heat the olive oil in a stockpot over medium-low heat. Add the carrot, celery, onion, bay leaves, garlic, and pepper. Cook, stirring often, for about 2 minutes. Add the water, tomato puree, potato, chopped clams, clam juice, and clam base. Bring to a boil, then reduce the heat to a low simmer. Cover the pot and let the soup cook for 20 to 25 minutes.

To serve, ladle the Manhattan Clam Chowder into individual serving bowls. Garnish with some chopped parsley and serve.

SUGGESTED PAIRING:

Boutari "Santorini" Assyrtiko, Santorini, Greece

The vineyard of Santorini is—at three hundred years of age—one of the oldest in Greece. The vines are not grafted on American rootstocks because phylloxera (vine louse) has never attacked the island. Brilliant, pale yellow in color, and featuring a pleasant distinctive aroma of citrus fruits, this fatty wine has very good balance and a full taste of figs and plums with a long aromatic aftertaste.

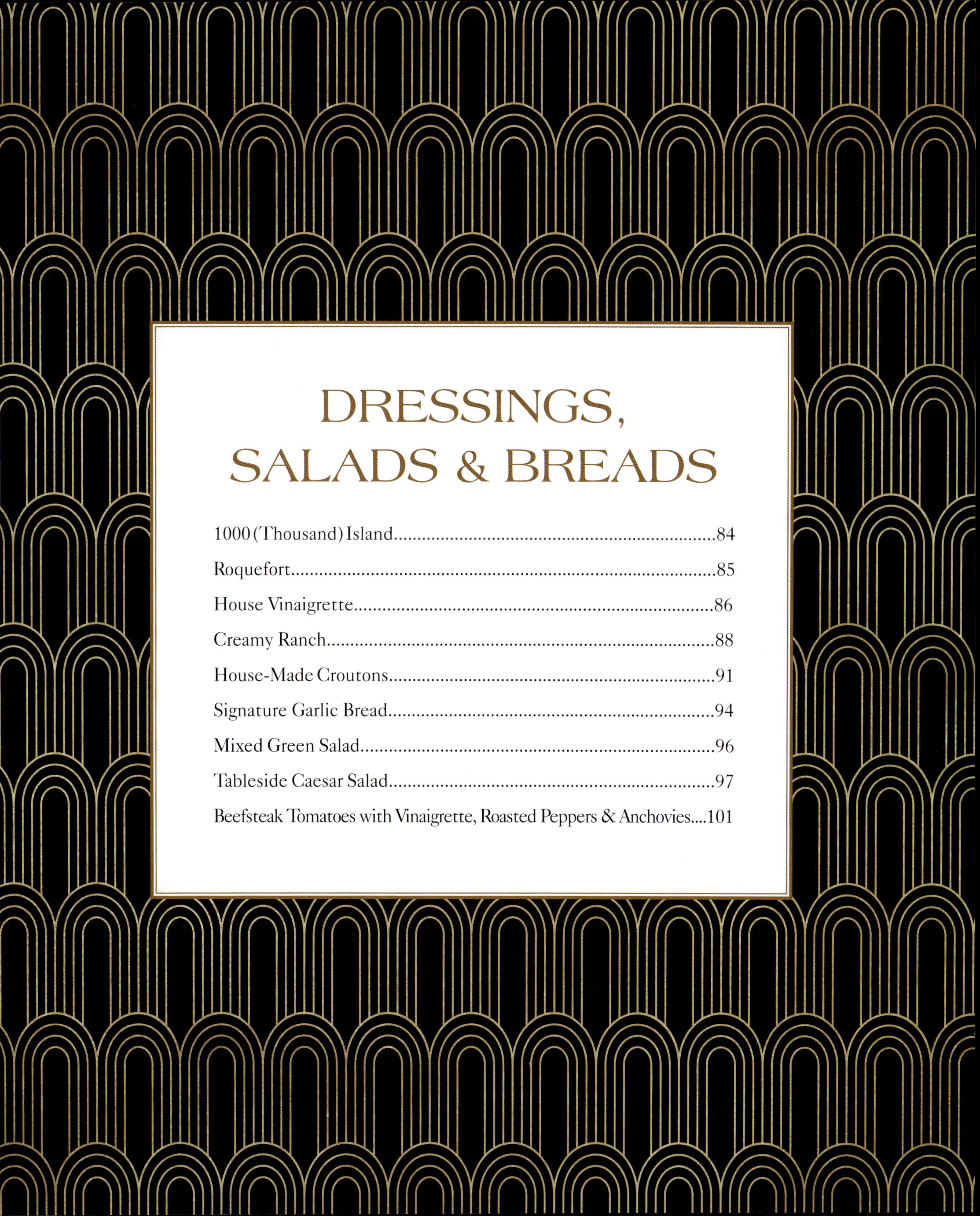

DRESSINGS, SALADS & BREADS

1000 (Thousand) Island....84

Roquefort....85

House Vinaigrette....86

Creamy Ranch....88

House-Made Croutons....91

Signature Garlic Bread....94

Mixed Green Salad....96

Tableside Caesar Salad....97

Beefsteak Tomatoes with Vinaigrette, Roasted Peppers & Anchovies....101

1000 (THOUSAND) ISLAND

Makes about 2 cups

- 2 tablespoons sweet relish
- ½ teaspoon white pepper
- 3 tablespoons California sweet chili sauce (Heinz)
- 1 hard-boiled egg, peeled and diced
- 1 teaspoon Worcestershire sauce
- 2 cups mayonnaise

Named after the Thousand Islands region between the United States and Canada, 1000 (Thousand) Island Dressing dates back to the early 1900s—although there are conflicting stories of who actually created this mayonnaise-based condiment. In the 1950s—especially 1958 when the Golden Steer Steakhouse first opened its doors—Thousand Island Dressing was quite popular, and still is. In this recipe, the Steer chefs opt to use sweet relish instead of chopped pickles and also add chili sauce for a bit more zing.

In a mixing bowl, combine the relish, pepper, chili sauce, egg, Worcestershire, and mayonnaise. Whisk until smooth and creamy. Refrigerate until ready to use.

ROQUEFORT

This is an old-school dressing, popular in the 1970's but not mentioned much these days... unless you happen to be dining at an iconic restaurant like the Golden Steer Steakhouse. Roquefort is actually a sheep's-milk blue cheese from southern France. This cheese makes a bold dressing to top a wedge of iceberg or a simple mixed green salad. If you can't find Roquefort blue cheese, select a similar-quality blue cheese that's white, crumbly, slightly moist, and has the distinctive veins of the blue mold that gives the cheese its sharp tang.

In a mixing bowl, combine the Worcestershire, pepper, garlic, parsley, blue cheese, lemon juice, mayonnaise, and buttermilk. Whisk until smooth and creamy. Refrigerate until ready to use.

Makes about 2 cups

- ½ teaspoon Worcestershire sauce
- ½ teaspoon white pepper
- ½ teaspoon minced garlic
- ½ teaspoon chopped fresh Italian parsley
- 2 tablespoons crumbled Roquefort blue cheese
- ½ squeezed lemon juice
- 1½ cup mayonnaise
- ½ cup low-fat buttermilk

HOUSE VINAIGRETTE

Makes about 2 cups

- ½ teaspoon salt
- 1 teaspoon ground mustard
- 1 teaspoon dried oregano
- ½ teaspoon white pepper
- ½ teaspoon sugar
- ½ teaspoon minced garlic
- ½ cup red wine vinegar
- 1 cup California chili sauce (Heinz)
- ½ cup canola oil

Combine oil with an acid, such as vinegar or citrus, and you have the building blocks used in most vinaigrettes. At the Golden Steer Steakhouse, canola oil is used with red wine vinegar in a 2:1 ratio. The dressing is then enhanced with salt and seasonings along with some fresh garlic. What makes the Golden Steer House Vinaigrette different from many other vinaigrettes is the addition of a spicy red chili sauce made from vine-ripened fresh California tomatoes. This adds a touch of sweetness and stability to the delicious emulsified dressing. (It's the same chili sauce used in Golden Steer Steakhouse's Cocktail Sauce, page 54).

In a mixing bowl, blend the salt, mustard, oregano, pepper, garlic, and vinegar. Whisk until combined. Add the chili sauce and oil, and continue whisking until incorporated. Refrigerate until ready to use.

CREAMY RANCH

Makes about 2 cups

- 1 cup mayonnaise
- 1 cup low-fat buttermilk
- 2 teaspoons Hidden Valley Dry Seasoning Mix
- ½ teaspoon chopped fresh Italian parsley

Combine buttermilk, herbs, and mayonnaise and you have what has been the best-selling salad dressing since 1993, when ranch finally surpassed Italian as the dressing of choice in America. Steve and Gayle Henson, who opened Hidden Valley Ranch outside Santa Barbara, California, served their original creation to guests staying at the ranch in the mid-1950s. Twenty years later, the Hensons cashed in and sold their handcrafted dressing for millions. Today the Golden Steer Steakhouse incorporates a bit of history into its Creamy Ranch. Chefs add to their buttermilk a few teaspoons of Hidden Valley Dry Seasoning Mix—the same mix the Hensons sold to their guests so they could go home and mix their own dressing. If it's not broke, don't fix it, and that's exactly what the Steer chefs do when it comes to making their Creamy Ranch Dressing.

In a mixing bowl, combine the mayonnaise, buttermilk, seasoning mix, and parsley. Whisk until smooth and creamy. Refrigerate until ready to use.

HOUSE-MADE CROUTONS

It's surprising how much better homemade croutons are than store-bought. Most store-bought croutons are hard and dry, and don't have the taste a homemade crouton boasts. The Golden Steer Steakhouse makes croutons weekly, and they're so easy. These croutons are featured in the Golden Steer's Tableside Caesar Salad.

- White bread, cubed into 1-inch pieces
- Paprika
- Fresh-grated Parmesan cheese
- Garlic powder
- Canola oil

Preheat the oven to 400°F.

Put the white bread cubes in a mixing bowl. Sprinkle generously with paprika, Parmesan cheese, and garlic powder. Drizzle with some canola oil, and toss until the bread is evenly coated. Arrange evenly on a sheet pan and place in the oven for about 10 minutes, or until crispy. Remove the croutons from the oven and let them cool. Store in a sealed container until ready to use.

SIGNATURE GARLIC BREAD

- 1 French bread loaf, sliced 1-inch thick on the bias
- Garlic-Infused Oil (recipe follows)
- Garlic Butter (recipe follows)
- Parmesan Cheese Mixture (recipe follows)

As noted on the Golden Steer Steakhouse dinner menu, Signature Garlic Bread is made fresh daily with imported cheese. Although variations of the basic garlic bread—bread baked with garlic, oil, and herbs—are found across America, the secret to the Steer's version is the perfect combination of Garlic-Infused Oil, Garlic Butter, and a Parmesan Cheese Mixture that, when schmeared on top, creates a crunchy bread of outrageous deliciousness.

Preheat the oven to 400°F.

The first step is to dip one side of a bread slice into the Garlic-Infused Oil (recipe follows). Next, spread an even layer of Garlic Butter (recipe follows) on the oiled side, then finally dip into the Parmesan Cheese Mixture (recipe follows). Transfer the bread to a baking sheet and repeat the process with the remaining slices. Bake for 1 or 2 minutes, or until golden brown.

GARLIC-INFUSED OIL

- 2 teaspoons minced garlic
- ½ cup olive oil

In a mixing bowl, combine the garlic and olive oil. Reserve until ready to use.

GARLIC BUTTER

- 1 cup softened butter
- ½ cup fresh-grated Parmesan cheese
- 4 tablespoons minced garlic

In a mixing bowl, combine the butter, cheese, and garlic. Keep at room temperature until ready to use.

PARMESAN CHEESE MIXTURE

- ½ cup fresh-grated Parmesan cheese
- ½ teaspoon garlic powder
- 2 tablespoons chopped fresh Italian parsley

In a mixing bowl, combine the cheese, garlic powder, and parsley. Reserve until ready to use.

MIXED GREEN SALAD

Serves 1

- Iceberg lettuce
- Tomatoes
- Sliced cucumber
- Shaved carrots
- Garbanzo beans
- Dressing of choice (see Dressings)

The salad—mixed greens with dressing—dates back to ancient times. The Greeks and Romans ate salads that contained raw vegetables, often dressed with a little oil, vinegar, and herbs. As time progressed, salads became more complicated. The dinner salad served at the Golden Steer Steakhouse pays homage to the simple, easy-to-make, garden-fresh salad. As they say, do as the Romans do.

In a mixing bowl, combine the lettuce, tomatoes, cucumber, carrots, and garbanzo beans. Toss with your dressing of choice, and serve.

SUGGESTED PAIRING:

Antinori Guado al Tasso Vermentino
Bolgheri, Italy

The first Vermentino to be produced at the Guado al Tasso estate was the 1996. The property is located approximately fifty miles southwest of Florence near the medieval hamlet of Bolgheri in the Tuscan Maremma. Luminous straw yellow in color, the wine is elegant and rich with pleasant floral and citrus notes. This Vermentino is fruit-driven, fresh, and crisp, with a lingering minerality and bright fruity finish.

TABLESIDE CAESAR SALAD

Everyone who enjoys steaks or dines at steakhouses across America has probably had their fair share of Caesar salads. Created in the early 1920s by Italian restaurateur Caesar Cardini, the Caesar salad is not meant to be premade or made in bulk. In fact, most high-quality steakhouses, like the Golden Steer, choose to prepare their Caesar salad tableside in front of guests, who can also customize the salad dressing to their specific palate (such as more Worcestershire or less vinegar). This recipe is similar to Cardini's original, with the addition of a few ingredients to give the salad a zestier kick. For those with health concerns, the egg yolk can be optional.

Serves 2

- 1 teaspoon Dijon mustard
- ½ lemon, juiced
- 1 egg yolk
- 1 teaspoon red wine vinegar
- ½ teaspoon Worcestershire sauce
- ¼ teaspoon Tabasco hot sauce
- ½ tablespoon minced fresh anchovies
- ¾ tablespoon minced garlic
- ⅓ cup olive oil
- 1 tablespoon fresh-grated Parmesan cheese
- 1 head romaine lettuce, chopped
- House-Made Croutons (page 91)
- Parmesan cheese

In a large mixing bowl, combine the mustard, lemon juice, egg yolk, and vinegar. Whisk to blend. Add the Worcestershire, Tabasco, anchovies, and garlic. Continue to whisk until incorporated. Drizzle in the olive oil while whisking, and add the cheese to thicken the dressing. Add the romaine and House-Made Croutons; sprinkle generously with some more cheese. Toss well and serve.

SUGGESTED PAIRING:

Pascal Jolivet Sancerre Sauvignon Blanc, Loire, France

The house of Pascal Jolivet is one of the youngest and most dynamic in the Loire Valley. Founded in 1985, this specialist in the wines of Sancerre has very quickly gained a leading position with the Michelin-starred restaurants of France. Pale and vibrant in color, this Sancerre is fresh and clean, with racy acidity tempered by very subtle residual sugar. The palate is fresh and tightly wound. Overall, a dry and elegant wine.

BEEFSTEAK TOMATOES WITH VINAIGRETTE, ROASTED PEPPERS & ANCHOVIES

This salad is representative of the Golden Steer Steakhouse, and showcases large, juicy, full-flavored beefsteak tomatoes, which are perfect for eating fresh from the harvest. Beefsteaks are typically wide tomatoes, but the rounder varieties have a sweeter flavor. You can also substitute large heirloom tomatoes if the beefsteaks are not available. Although the dish served at the Steer highlights pimientos, roasted peppers are substituted here. The flavor is best if you roast the peppers yourself, but the jarred variety will work fine, too.

Serves 1

- 1 romaine lettuce leaf
- 1 beefsteak tomato, halved
- 1 roasted red bell pepper (page 57)
- 4 anchovy fillets
- House Vinaigrette (page 86)

Place the lettuce leaf on a serving plate. Add the two tomato halves. On top of each tomato, place half of the roasted red bell pepper. Arrange two anchovy fillets on top of each pepper. Finish with a drizzle of House Vinaigrette.

SUGGESTED PAIRING:

Sculpin IPA Beer, Ballast Point Brewing Company, San Diego, California

The Sculpin IPA is a great example of what got the brewers of Ballast Point into brewing in the first place. After years of experimenting, they knew hopping an ale at five separate stages would produce something special. The inspired use of hops creates hints of apricot, peach, mango, and lemon flavors, but still packs a bit of a sting, just like a sculpin fish.

FRANK'S MENU

For those who would like to dine like Frank Sinatra, the following menu lists the dishes the Chairman of the Board regularly ordered while he dined at the Golden Steer Steakhouse (all the recipes are featured in this book). Fellow Rat Packer Sammy Davis Jr. is credited with having introduced Frank to the Steer. In the 1960s, African Americans weren't allowed to dine inside Vegas hotels, including the Sands Hotel & Casino where Sammy and the Rat Pack performed. Because the Golden Steer welcomed Sammy and the Rat Pack, it became their preferred restaurant in Las Vegas. Today the Golden Steer Steakhouse remains one of the last remaining establishments in town where Frank and the Rat Pack dined before performing. Frank was even known for walking around the restaurant and serenading fellow guests while they ate and drank. If you're dining at the Golden Steer, you can still request one of three tables where the Rat Pack actually sat for dinner, all three next to one another: Sammy Davis Jr., Booth 20; Dean Martin, Booth 21; and Frank Sinatra, Booth 22.

PRE-DINNER COCKTAIL

Three fingers of Jack Daniel's served with two ice cubes

APPETIZER

Narragansett Bay Clams Casino (page 56)

DINNER ENTRÉE

16-ounce New York Strip (served medium-rare) with Pizzaiola Sauce (page 118)

SUGGESTED PAIRING

Grgich Wine Estates Merlot, Napa Valley, California

Mike Grgich first gained international recognition at the celebrated Paris Tasting of 1976, in which a panel of eminent French judges swirled, sniffed, and sipped an array of the fabled white Burgundies of France and a small sampling of upstart Chardonnays from the Napa Valley. When the results were in, the French judges were shocked: They had chosen Mike's 1973 Montelena Chardonnay as the finest white wine in the world. This Merlot offers complex flavors of red currant, black licorice, and a hint of savory herbs wrapped in a velvety texture. The firm tannins and acidity make it the perfect partner for prime ribeye steak.

DESSERT

Bananas Foster (page 208)

PRIME AGED BEEF & CHOPS

Rib Eye with Bone In....110

Filet Mignon....112

Filet Mignon with Lobster Tail....113

Filet Mignon Oscar-Style....117

New York Strip with Pizzaiola Sauce....118

T-Bone....122

Prime Rib of Beef....124

Châteaubriand for Two....129

Double-Cut American Lamb Chops....130

Porterhouse-Cut Pork Chop....133

RIB EYE WITH BONE IN

Serves 1

- 1 22-ounce bone-in prime rib eye steak
- Lawry's Seasoned Salt
- ¼ cup House-Made Beef Stock (page 68, optional)

Some guests at the Golden Steer Steakhouse swear by a New York strip or a T-bone; some are die-hard for the Prime Rib of Beef, while others won't touch anything but a filet mignon. But there are many patrons who believe the ultimate steak is the Steer's rich, beefy twenty-two ounce bone-in rib eye. The rib eye is cut from ribs six through twelve on the cow, between the loin and the shoulder. If you come across a rib eye without the bone, it's usually referred to as Delmonico. The rib eye is the most marbled of the high-end steaks, which means it has the most flavor. It's also the most prone to flare-ups on the grill, so make sure you don't walk away when this steak is sizzling.

Lightly season the rib eye steak with the seasoned salt. Place on a prepared outdoor grill or under the broiler, and cook until your desired internal temperature is achieved, about 6 minutes on each side, for medium-rare. Remove from the heat and let rest for 5 to 10 minutes. Plate and serve with the House-Made Beef Stock over the top, if desired.

SUGGESTED PAIRING:

Grgich Wine Estates Merlot,
Napa Valley, California

Mike Grgich first gained international recognition at the celebrated Paris Tasting of 1976, in which a panel of eminent French judges swirled, sniffed, and sipped an array of the fabled white Burgundies of France and a small sampling of upstart Chardonnays from the Napa Valley. When the results were in, the French judges were shocked: They had chosen Mike's 1973 Montelena Chardonnay as the finest white wine in the world. This Merlot offers complex flavors of red currant, black licorice, and a hint of savory herbs wrapped in a velvety texture. The firm tannins and acidity make it the perfect partner for prime rib-eye steak.

FILET MIGNON

Serves 1

- 1 8- or 12-ounce prime filet mignon
- Lawry's Seasoned Salt
- ¼ cup House-Made Beef Stock (page 68, optional)

Also known as the tenderloin, this boneless cut is the most tender and the most sought-after despite its subtle beef flavor. It comes from the tenderloin, which lies in the middle of the cow's back. Because this muscle is not overly exerted, the tendons do not toughen, creating a lean yet succulent steak that has an elegance about it with its buttery texture and compact shape. The filet is arguably the most requested cut at steak houses across America, including the Golden Steer, which has dubbed this steak the Aristocrat of Tenderness. At the Steer, it's served in two sizes: eight ounces (petite) and twelve ounces.

Lightly season the filet mignon with the seasoned salt. Place on a prepared outdoor grill or under the broiler, and cook until your desired internal temperature is achieved, about 4 to 5 minutes on each side, for medium-rare. Remove from the heat and plate. Serve with the House-Made Beef Stock over the top, if desired.

SUGGESTED PAIRING:

Château d'Agassac Haut-Médoc
Bordeaux, France

This estate's two greatest assets are the quality of its terroir and its precious stock of old vines. The terroir, with its warm soils made up of deep, well-drained gravels and copious amounts of sunshine, is distinguished by its early-maturing character—Agassac is often the first estate in the area to begin harvesting. Structured and well balanced, the nose of this Bordeaux emerges in layers of floral notes. Dense tannin and a long finish pleasantly follow, with hints of cayenne pepper and clove supported by graphite and chalk notes of the terroir.

FILET MIGNON WITH LOBSTER TAIL

Similar to the Filet Mignon Oscar-Style, this Golden Steer Steakhouse recipe also incorporates fresh seafood to complement its beef. Most steak houses across America refer to this combination as surf 'n' turf—a term coined in the early 1960s for combining seafood with red meat, which ironically was served to the middle class because of its affordability. Today at the Steer, chefs pair their petite filet and New York strip with a large 12-ounce Western Australian Lobster Tail for a mouthwatering combination dinner, which is accompanied by a choice of the Golden Steer Mixed Green Salad or soup *du jour*, and the vegetable of the day.

Note: You can substitute Alaskan King Crab Legs (page 141) or Shrimp Scampi (page 138) for the lobster tail; the Golden Steer Steakhouse offers these as combination dinners, too.

Serves 1

- 1 8-ounce prime filet mignon (or New York strip)
- Lawry's Seasoned Salt
- 1 Jumbo Western Australian Lobster Tail, 12 ounces (page 140)
- ¼ cup House-Made Beef Stock (page 68, optional)

Lightly season the filet mignon with the seasoned salt. Place on a prepared outdoor grill or under the broiler, and cook until desired internal temperature is achieved, about 4 to 5 minutes on each side, for medium-rare. Remove from the heat and plate. Serve with the House-Made Beef Stock over the top, if desired.

SUGGESTED PAIRING:

Stags' Leap Winery Petite Sirah,
Napa Valley, California

A fashionable country resort in the mid-twentieth century, popular with Hollywood due to its 1892 stone manor house and historic gardens, along with its legends of bootleggers and gangsters, ghosts and gypsies, Stags' Leap has been home to three major family groups up through the modern revitalization of the winery that began in the 1970s. This Petite Sirah is deeply colored and is a classic example of the full-bodied, rich varietal. Notes of blackberry, black cherry, and mulberry, as well as subtle hints of rose tea, vanilla, graphite, clove spice, and sweet tobacco, permeate throughout, as this wine exhibits the full spectrum of Petite Sirah's signature characteristics.

FILET MIGNON OSCAR-STYLE

This culinary creation dates back to the mid-1800s during the reign of Sweden's King Oscar II, who enjoyed veal topped with crab or crayfish meat, Béarnaise sauce, and garnished with asparagus spears. Today you will find filet mignon being crowned with cooked asparagus, crabmeat, and a dollop of Hollandaise. Some claim this variation on King Oscar's dish is actually named in honor of Oscar Tschirky from The Waldorf Astoria in New York. Whichever Oscar it's really named after, this flavorful recipe is best served with a filet, because the tenderloin is not as flavorful as other high-end cuts of beef and the Oscar helps to enhance the flavor profile of the meat. The Golden Steer Steakhouse serves Filet Mignon Oscar with succulent Alaskan king crab and house-made Hollandaise Sauce. If you're unable to obtain Alaskan king crab, simply use another premium crab meat, such as Dungeness.

Serves 1

- 1 8 or 12-ounce prime filet mignon
- Lawry's Seasoned Salt
- 1 cooked asparagus spear (page 188), cut into thirds
- 1 tablespoon Alaskan king crabmeat (or other premium crabmeat)
- 1 dollop Hollandaise Sauce (page 200)
- Chopped fresh Italian parsley, for garnish

Lightly season the filet mignon with the seasoned salt. Place on a prepared outdoor grill or under the broiler, and cook until your desired internal temperature is achieved, about 4 to 5 minutes on each side, for medium-rare. Remove from the heat and plate. Arrange the cut asparagus on top of the steak, followed by the crabmeat on top of the asparagus, and the Hollandaise Sauce over the crab. Garnish with a sprinkle of fresh parsley.

SUGGESTED PAIRING:

Paraduxx Napa Valley Proprietary Red Wine, Napa Valley, California

From the only winery devoted to stylish Napa Valley blends, the Paraduxx Proprietary Red is a bold and expressive blend of Cabernet, Merlot, Zinfandel, and Petit Verdot, crafted to satisfy the modern palate. The wine has rich, full fruit flavors and soft, elegant tannins. The nose offers deep, concentrated aromas of blackberry cobbler and rich brambly fruit. The palate is soft and rich, with balanced tannins framing lush layers of blueberry, blackberry, and spice, all of which carry through to a long, supple finish.

NEW YORK STRIP WITH PIZZAIOLA SAUCE

Serves 1

- 1 16-ounce prime New York strip steak
- Lawry's Seasoned Salt
- Pizzaiola Sauce (recipe follows)

The New York strip, as it's referred to outside New York (it's simply strip steak to New Yorkers or Kanas City strip to Kansans), is a moderately tender cut of beef with good marbling and beefy flavor from the short loin of the cow. The Golden Steer Steakhouse serves its 16-ounce cut without the bone. This also happened to be Frank Sinatra's favorite steak, which he preferred medium-rare and always topped with Golden Steer Steakhouse's house-made Pizzaiola Sauce. Elvis, who happened to be the longest tenured guest at the Golden Steer Steakhouse, would devour two or three New Yorks in one sitting before his performance on stage.

Lightly season the New York strip with the seasoned salt. Place it on a prepared outdoor grill or under the broiler, and cook until your desired internal temperature is achieved, about 4 to 5 minutes on each side, for medium-rare. Remove from the heat and let rest for 5 to 10 minutes. Plate and serve with Pizzaiola Sauce (or Peppercorn Sauce, page 198, for Andretti fans) over the top.

PIZZAIOLA SAUCE

- ½ tablespoon canola oil
- ½ beefsteak tomato, chopped large
- ½ teaspoon minced garlic
- 1 pinch salt
- 1 pinch white pepper
- ½ tablespoon salted butter
- 1 tablespoon Marinara Sauce (page 157)
- ½ tablespoon white wine
- 1 pinch oregano
- ½ teaspoon Roux (page 73)
- ½ teaspoon chopped fresh Italian parsley

Heat the oil in a sauté pan over medium heat. Add the tomato, garlic, salt, pepper, and butter. Toss well to combine, and cook for about 1 minute. Add the Marinara Sauce, white wine, and oregano, and cook for about 3 minutes. Add the Roux to reduce the water in the pan. Cook for 1 or 2 minutes, or until the tomato is soft and the liquid is the consistency of a thin sauce. Remove from the heat, sprinkle with parsley, and serve atop the steak.

SUGGESTED PAIRING:

Banfi Brunello di Montalcino, Sangiovese, Italy

In 1978, John and Harry Mariani, owners of the US wine importer Banfi Vintners, established the award-winning vineyard estate and winery Castello Banfi in the Brunello region of Tuscany. This extraordinary property is a constellation of single vineyards located on ideal sites that cover about one-third of the seventy-one-hundred-acre estate. Ruby red with aromas of violets and vanilla and hints of licorice, this exquisite Sangiovese offers a velvety palate with tart cherry flavors and traces of spice, along with supple tannins, good acidity, and a long finish.

T-BONE

Serves 1

- 1 20-ounce prime T-bone steak
- Lawry's Seasoned Salt
- ¼ cup House-Made Beef Stock (page 68, optional)

When you're looking for an ideal steak to grill, the Golden Steer Steakhouse's generous twenty-ounce T-bone (a bone-in strip and filet mignon) is a traditional favorite for serious steak lovers looking for two prized cuts of beef in one. Named after the T-shaped bone with meat on each side, the T-bone is often moderately marbled and contains a smaller filet whereas the Porterhouse steak offers a larger filet. Because you're essentially getting two steaks in one, the T-bone (and Porterhouse) is considered one of the highest-quality steaks on the market.

Lightly season the T-bone steak with the seasoned salt. Place on a prepared outdoor grill or under the broiler, and cook until your desired internal temperature is achieved, about 4 to 5 minutes on each side, for medium-rare. Remove from the heat and plate. Serve with the House-Made Beef Stock over the top, if desired.

SUGGESTED PAIRING:

Jordan Alexander Valley Cabernet Sauvignon, Sonoma, California

In 1972, Tom and Sally Jordan, a young couple from Colorado who shared an unbridled enthusiasm for French food and wine, followed their hearts to California's esteemed wine country. Since their inaugural 1976 vintage, the Jordans have been heralded for their elegant wines, culinary excellence, and gracious hospitality. Expect to find in this Cabernet blend concentrated aromas of blackberries and black cherries with an inviting hint of cedar. The wine's silky palate is long and expansive, boasting a beautiful balance of black fruit, fine tannin, and long finish.

PRIME RIB OF BEEF

Serves 9–14

- 1 20-pound, 9-rib prime-grade prime rib
- Au Jus (page 68)
- Horseradish-Cream Sauce (recipe follows)

This king of cuts claims center stage during the holiday season given its massive amounts of rich, juicy, tender beef that is perfectly marbled and relatively easy to cook. Unlike other prime cuts of beef, purchasing a USDA-prime cut of prime rib often means special-ordering the roast from your local butcher. But the cost is well worth it, as a prime-grade prime rib offers more marbling throughout, increasing its rich and tender beefy flavor. At the Golden Steer Steakhouse, chefs daily cook 20-pound roasts—which, surprisingly, aren't pre-seasoned with any salt and pepper. The chefs prefer to let the meat do all the talking. Each roast serves nine to fourteen guests, depending on the portion size. The Steer offers three different cuts: Diamond Jim Cut (24 ounces), Diamond Lil Cut (18 ounces), and English Cut (10 ounces), all served with its Au Jus and Horseradish-Cream Sauce made in-house. Football great and now convicted felon O. J. Simpson preferred the Diamond Jim cut at the Steer, which happened to be the last meal the "Juice" enjoyed as a free man before being arrested the next day in Las Vegas for numerous felonies connected with an alleged armed robbery at the Palace Station Hotel & Casino.

Preheat the oven to 300°F.

Transfer the prime rib, fat-side up and rib-bones down, to a roasting pan and bake for 2 hours. Remove from the oven and let rest for 15 minutes before slicing. Cooking a 20-pound roast for 2 hours at 300°F should result in cuts of rare, medium-rare, medium, and medium-well, which are the end cuts. Remember, you can always put the roast back in the oven if it's too rare for your taste. Just make sure you don't overcook it. For a thicker crust, yes, you can cover the prime rib with coarse salt. After removing it from the oven, let the salt-coated roast rest for about 30 minutes before carving (always slice across the grain). Be aware that the roast will continue to cook while resting. Serve with Au Jus and/or Horseradish-Cream Sauce.

HORSERADISH-CREAM SAUCE

Makes about 4 cups

- 4 cups sour cream
- 3 tablespoons fresh-grated horseradish
- 1 tablespoon Worcestershire sauce

In a mixing bowl, combine the sour cream, horseradish, and Worcestershire. Whisk until smooth and creamy. Refrigerate until ready to use, or up to 3 days.

SUGGESTED PAIRING:

Justin Isosceles Cabernet Sauvignon, Central Coast, California

Justin and Deborah Baldwin acquired their land in 1981. In 1987, they harvested their first grapes bottled under the Justin label. Isoscleles is a 100 percent estate blend of Cabernet Sauvignon, Merlot, and Cabernet Franc. Varietals are planted to specific soil types on their hillside vineyards eight miles from the Pacific Ocean, on the Central Coast. Intense and complex aromas of ripe black fruit, baking spice, leather, and cocoa make up the Isosceles. A dry and full-bodied wine, Isosceles is rich in black cherry and blackcurrant fruit, vanilla, cinnamon, and licorice notes. The finish is very long and complex, framed by soft, chewy tannins.

CHÂTEAUBRIAND FOR TWO

The châteaubriand, for those unfamiliar, is not a particular cut of beef, but rather a French term for the preparation of a roast from the center section of the beef tenderloin. It is often seen on steakhouse menus, including that of the Golden Steer Steakhouse, as Châteaubriand for Two because of the large portion (twenty-four ounces is what you'll find at the Steer). Terry Fator, famed Las Vegas ventriloquist, impressionist, and comedian, orders the châteaubriand at the Golden Steer Steakhouse two or three times a week. He also happens to be one of the last guests to leave the restaurant, and he always leaves satisfied and with plenty of leftovers. At the Steer, the tuxedo-clad captains carve the châteaubriand tableside for the guests; it's accompanied by a medley of fresh-cooked vegetables and both Béarnaise and Hollandaise Sauce.

Serves 2

- 1 24-ounce center-cut prime beef tenderloin
- Lawry's Seasoned Salt
- Vegetables (page 188)
- Béarnaise Sauce (page 201)
- Hollandaise Sauce (page200)

Preheat the oven to 350°F.

Lightly season the beef tenderloin with the seasoned salt. Bake in the oven until your desired internal temperature is achieved, about 15 minutes, for medium-rare. Remove from the heat and let rest for 15 minutes. Transfer the beef tenderloin to a cutting board atop a serving platter. Slice tableside and serve with a side of vegetables, Béarnaise Sauce, and Hollandaise Sauce.

SUGGESTED PAIRING:

Quintessa Cabernet Blend,
Napa Valley, California

The Quintessa estate is one of the most scenic and geographically unusual properties of the Napa Valley. Agustin and Valeria Huneeus began to develop the property as a vineyard in 1990. Keeping with her vision as steward of this land, she's guided Quintessa's evolution from sustainable farming in 1990 to biodynamic farming in 2000. The Cabernet Blend's forward fruit and supple, silky texture enrobe the palate with cola and nutmeg notes, filling out deeply layered black fruit flavors. The finish is rich, dense, and refined, lifted by ample lingering fruit.

DOUBLE-CUT AMERICAN LAMB CHOPS

Serves 2–3

- 1 2-pound American lamb rack (Frenched 8-bone)
- Lawry's Seasoned Salt
- Pineapple rings, for garnish
- Mint jelly

American lamb chops, which come from the rib, loin, sirloin, and shoulder of a US-raised lamb that likely has been grain-fed, have a delicate flavor and tenderness unlike the Australian and New Zealand cuts. At the Golden Steer Steakhouse, chefs cook whole two-pound Frenched eight-bone racks, which is equivalent to eight chops per rack. However, the Steer serves double-cut style, so you're getting four chops per rack. (Note: When lamb is portioned, the cuts become "chops," not "steaks.") The term *Frenched* refers to a lamb rack in which a few inches of meat have been removed from the end of the bones. Lamb chops, which remain an icon of fine-dining establishments across the country, are surprisingly easy to prepare at home while making for an impressive presentation, especially when you're entertaining.

Preheat the oven to 350°F.

Lightly season the lamb chops with the seasoned salt. Place in the oven and bake until your desired internal temperature is achieved, about 17 minutes, for medium-rare. Remove from the oven and let rest for 10 minutes before slicing and serving. To plate, portion three double-cut lamb chops per serving. Garnish with pineapple rings and a side of mint jelly.

SUGGESTED PAIRING:

Guigal Châteauneuf-du-Pape Rhône Valley Blend, Rhône, France

The Guigal domain was founded in 1946 by Etienne Guigal in the ancient village of Ampuis, home of the wines of the Côte-Rôtie. In these vineyards that are over twenty-four hundred years old, you can still see the small terraced walls characteristic of the Roman period. The Rhône Valley Blend comprises Grenache, Syrah, and Mourvedre.

PORTERHOUSE-CUT PORK CHOP

Another name for a bone-in loin pork chop, the Porterhouse cut derives its name from the Porterhouse steak for easier identification and preparation. This particular pork chop with its T-shaped bone is a very lean center cut from the hip and loin toward the back of the animal. Depending on where they're cut from, the chops may contain some pieces of tenderloin (hence the name *Porterhouse*). The large Porterhouse chops served at the Golden Steer Steakhouse include plenty of tenderloin, which adds to the very mild and delicious pork flavor. The secret to serving moist pork chops is to cook them quickly while still cooking them through. If you're using a meat thermometer, cook until you get an internal temperature around 150°F.

Serves 1

- 1 1½-pound Porterhouse (bone-in loin) pork chop
- Lawry's Seasoned Salt

Preheat the oven to 350°F.

Lightly season the pork chops with the seasoned salt. Place in the oven and bake until cooked through, being careful not to overcook, about 15 minutes. Remove from the plate and serve.

SUGGESTED PAIRING:

Benton-Lane First Class Pinot Noir,
Willamette Valley, Oregon

Steve and Carol Girard have been owners of Benton-Lane since 1988. Carol and Steve shared a passionate desire to produce great Pinot Noir, but decided their native California was probably not the best place in which to make it. Instead they headed to Oregon, where the cooler climate offered the possibility of producing Pinot Noir with better balance and structure. The dark rosewood color of this wine is accentuated by its tantalizing aromas. The dominant fruit scents favor black plums, currants, and other darker fruits, with more complex aromas of graphite and smoked meats as well. On the palate, you'll find savory flavors of mocha and Italian herbs, rounded out by fruity nuances of black raspberries and Van cherries.

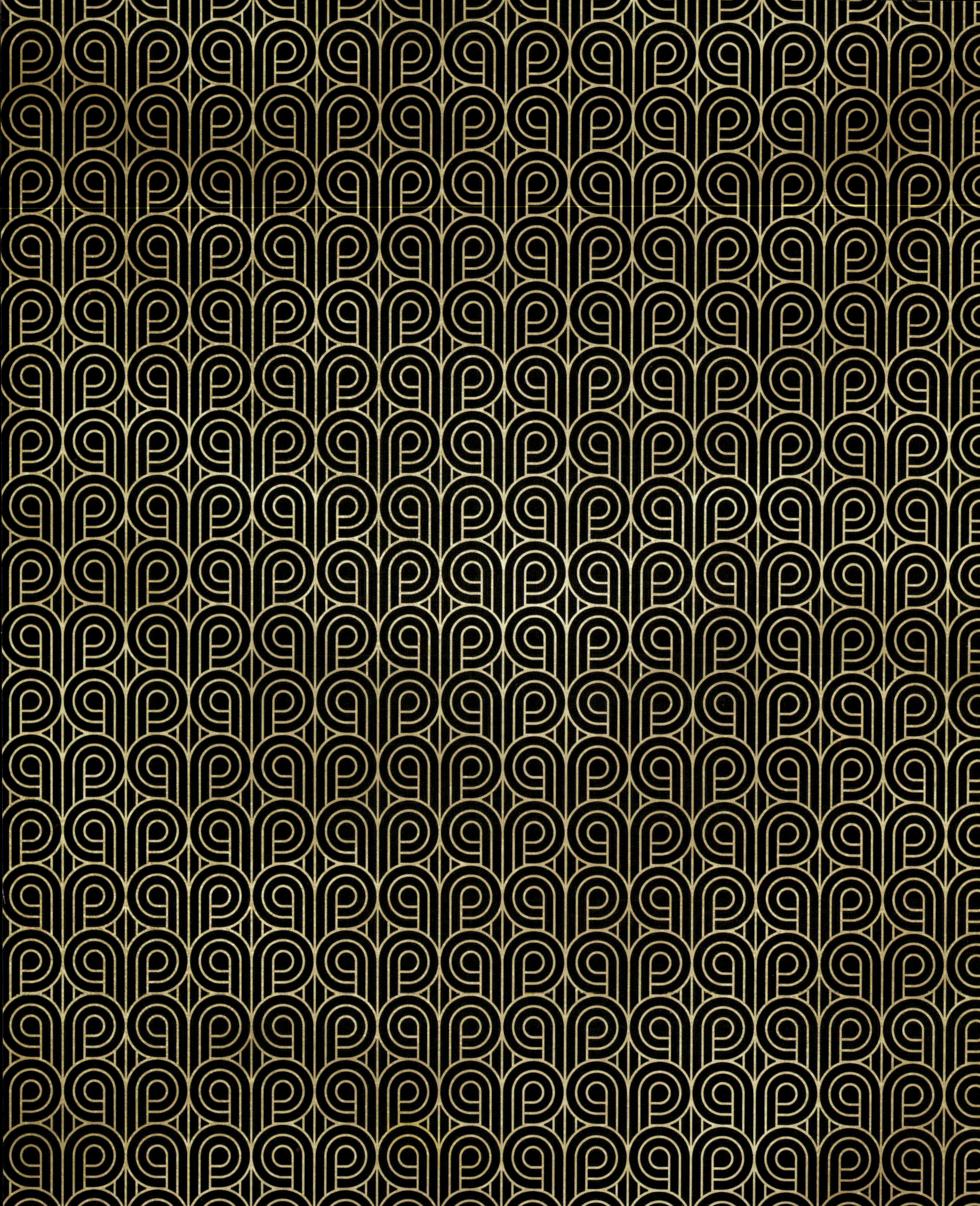

SEAFOOD

Shrimp Scampi with Mediterranean Sauce....138

Jumbo Western Australian Lobster Tail....140

Alaskan King Crab Legs....141

Blackened Alaskan Salmon....143

Baked Alaskan Salmon....144

Poached Alaskan Salmon with Dill Sauce....145

Dover Sole in Lemon Butter....146

SHRIMP SCAMPI WITH MEDITERRANEAN SAUCE

Serves 1

- 2 tablespoons olive oil
- 5 large wild-caught white jumbo Gulf shrimp, peeled and de-veined, tails intact
- 2 teaspoons salted butter
- 1 pinch salt
- 1 pinch white pepper
- 1 pinch oregano
- 3–4 dashes Worcestershire sauce
- 1 teaspoon white wine
- ½ lemon, juiced
- ¼ cup House-Made Chicken Stock (page 69)
- ½ teaspoon Roux (page 73)
- Chopped fresh Italian parsley, for garnish

Like the Jumbo Gulf Shrimp Cocktail, this recipe imbued with the taste of the Mediterranean calls for large grade-A wild-caught shrimp from the United States, close to the Gulf of Mexico. These shrimp are tastier, more tender and, most important, fresher than those foreign—and not so sustainable—imports. The texture of Gulf shrimp is also generally firmer than the pond-raised variety. For this dish, Golden Steer Steakhouse chefs prefer the white Gulf shrimp, rather than the brown or pink shrimp; these have a sweeter flavor with a firm, slightly "crunchy" texture.

Heat the olive oil in a sauté pan over medium heat. Add the shrimp and cook for 2 to 3 minutes. Turn the shrimp, and cook for another 2 to 3 minutes. Remove from the heat and drain the oil. Return the pan to the heat and add the butter, salt, pepper, oregano, Worcestershire, white wine, lemon juice, Chicken Stock, and Roux. Stir well to incorporate and continue to cook until the sauce is creamy and the shrimp are cooked through. Remove from the heat. Arrange the shrimp on a serving plate, and ladle the sauce over the top. Garnish with fresh parsley and serve.

SUGGESTED PAIRING:

Ferrari-Carano Chardonnay,
Sonoma, California

Ferrari-Carano in Sonoma County offers superior lots of wine from vineyards in Alexander Valley, Dry Creek Valley, Russian River Valley, and Carneros. This full-bodied yet refreshing Chardonnay boasts aromas of lemon, pear, green apple, orange blossom, and vanilla with a beautiful floral finish.

JUMBO WESTERN AUSTRALIAN LOBSTER TAIL

Serves 1

- 1 12-ounce Australian western rock lobster tail
- 1 pinch paprika
- 4 tablespoons melted salted butter, divided

The lobster tails at the Golden Steer Steakhouse are enormous at twelve ounces each. They come from Australia's western rock lobster. These spiny lobsters don't have the large claws of the cold-water Maine (American) lobsters. The western rock lobster also happens to be the most valuable single-species fishery in Australia at an estimated value of more than $200 million each year. It's evident the Golden Steer Steakhouse spares no expense when it comes to offering its guests some of the finest lobster on the planet.

Preheat the oven to 350°F.

With a sharp kitchen knife, split the lobster tail in half lengthwise, slicing through the top shell, but being careful not to pierce the bottom shell. Remove the lobster meat and place it on top of the shell. Transfer to an ovenproof dish. Sprinkle the top of the lobster meat with paprika, and drizzle with 2 tablespoons of the melted butter. Then add a thin layer of water to the bottom of the pan.

Place the pan in the oven and bake for 10 minutes, or until the lobster is cooked through. Serve with a side of the remaining melted butter.

SUGGESTED PAIRING:

Far Niente Chardonnay, Napa Valley, California

One of California's oldest wineries, Far Niente was founded in 1885. The winery flourished until Prohibition, at which time it was abandoned and fell into complete disrepair. The stately stone shell of a winery was purchased in 1979 by Gil Nickel. During restoration, the original name, Far Niente—romantically translated to "without a care"—was found carved in stone on the front of the building, where it remains to this day. The Chardonnay opens with light tropical aromas, juicy citrus, and a layer of toasted oak. The wine progresses to a creamy, structured mid-palate, and the long finish has bright acidity with lingering citrus, toasted nut, and wet stone flavors.

ALASKAN KING CRAB LEGS

As explained in the Alaskan King Crab Cocktail recipe, king crab legs are immediately cooked and blast-frozen after being off-loaded alive from the saltwater holds of crabbing boats to preserve their fresh taste. Because of this, king crab legs need only to be adequately heated before eating. When you're purchasing, remember that one pound of king crab legs will typically feed one person. At the Golden Steer Steakhouse, each king crab leg weighs one pound, and the restaurant serves two legs per guest. That's a lot of crab. After the legs thaw in the refrigerator, the chefs split and heat them under the broiler with a little paprika and melted butter before they're served.

Serves 1

- 2 extra-large Alaskan king crab legs, about 1 pound per leg
- 1 pinch paprika
- 4 tablespoons melted salted butter, divided

Preheat the oven to 350°F.

With a sharp kitchen knife, cut the legs in half, then split in half lengthwise to expose the meat. Arrange the crab legs in an ovenproof dish. Sprinkle with paprika, and drizzle with 2 tablespoons of the butter. Pour a thin layer of water into the bottom of the pan.

Place in the oven and bake for 10 minutes. Serve with a side of the remaining melted butter.

SUGGESTED PAIRING:

Dr. Pauly-Bergweiler, Riesling Kabinett, Mosel, Germany

Dr. Pauly's grandfather Zacharias Bergweiler was for many decades one of the most respected wine growers on the Mosel. It was the grandfather's wine estate that Dr. Pauly took over while still a student, subsequently completing his doctorate and writing a thesis on the economic opportunities offered by the Mosel-Saar-Ruwer wine-growing region. Refreshing due to its individual slate stone notes, Dr. Pauly's Riesling is direct and complex at the same time with aromas of citrus fruits and rhubarb. The taste is well balanced in natural sweetness and acidity.

BLACKENED ALASKAN SALMON

If you like your fish (salmon) blackened, there's an easy cooking technique often associated with Cajun cuisine that recreates the taste of grilled food, blackened by the flames. The method is to cook the fish in a very hot cast iron skillet with melted butter and a blend of herbs and spices to achieve an authentic blackened flavor. There are now a number of quality blackening seasonings on the market to help enhance that blackened flavor. Old Bay Blackened Seasoning is one such brand; its mixture of spices includes celery seed, red pepper, salt, paprika, and sugar. Golden Steer Steakhouse chefs prefer to use Cajun seasoning, which is similar to blackened seasoning, but brings out more of the flavors of the Louisiana bayou country with a blend of spicy-hot peppers, onions, garlic, and herbs. Regardless of which spice you prefer, the secret to blackened fish is cooking in a dab of scalding-hot butter.

Serves 1

- 1 8-ounce wild Alaskan salmon fillet
- Cajun seasoning, for dusting
- 1 tablespoon salted butter
- Chopped fresh Italian parsley, for garnish
- Wild Rice (page 192)

Preheat the oven to 350°F.

Dust the salmon fillet in Cajun seasoning, shaking off the excess. Add to a cast-iron skillet or sauté pan with the butter. Place in the oven and bake for 5 to 6 minutes. Turn the fish over and cook for another 5 to 6 minutes. Remove from the oven and plate. Garnish with some parsley and serve with a side of Wild Rice.

SUGGESTED PAIRING:

Argyle Winery Pinot Noir, Oregon

With a climate similar to Burgundy in rainfall, sunlight hours, and other climate factors, the Willamette Valley is known for its Pinot Noir and Pinot Gris. Pinot Noir vines in Oregon produces wines that are fruit-forward yet complex, some with good ageability. Argyle's Pinot Noir unveils black cherry and cranberry embraced by toasted hazelnuts; vanilla along with firm tannins; and a long finish. The fruity flavors, juicy acidity, and silky texture are the result of aging the wine sixteen months in French oak.

BAKED ALASKAN SALMON

Serves 1

- ½ tablespoon olive oil
- ½ tablespoon salted butter
- 1 8-ounce wild Alaskan salmon fillet
- Flour, for dusting
- Chopped fresh Italian parsley, for garnish
- Wild Rice (page 192)

Alaska supplies more than half of all the wild-caught seafood in the United States. It's also home to the greatest wild salmon runs in the world, including its famous Copper River, and provides as much as 95 percent of North America's wild salmon. Golden Steer Steakhouse chefs are always on the lookout for fresh troll-caught Alaskan salmon, which they find superior with no comparison. With wild Alaskan salmon, you get what you pay for—quality. And when it comes to Alaskan salmon, there are a handful of varieties to choose from: Chinook or king (the largest, with big meaty flakes), sockeye (considered the money fish in the salmon business because of its radiant color and healthy rich fat content), coho or silver (not as highly regarded as the king or sockeye, but a great salmon for the money), and the chum and pink species, both often reserved for canned or smoked salmon. Regardless of which salmon you select, make sure it's fresh, troll-caught, and from Alaska whenever possible.

Preheat the oven to 350°F.

Heat the olive oil and butter in a sauté pan over medium heat. Dust the salmon fillet in flour, shaking off the excess. Add it to the pan and cook until golden brown, about 1 to 2 minutes. Turn the fish over and remove from the heat. Transfer to the oven and bake for 5 to 6 minutes. Remove from the oven and plate. Garnish with some parsley and serve with a side of Wild Rice.

SUGGESTED PAIRING:

EnRoute Pinot Noir, Sonoma, California

EnRoute was established in the Russian River Valley in 2007 by the partners of Napa Valley's Far Niente winery. Devoted to producing Russian River Valley Pinot Noir, EnRoute introduced its first wine, Les Pommiers, in May 2009. Les Pommiers is named after the apple orchards that once flourished in the region. EnRoute's Pinot Noir showcases explosive aromatics of pomegranate and cherry with hints of perfume, tobacco leaf, mineral, baking spices, and a floral note with rich layered tannins and a finish that's bright and juicy.

POACHED ALASKAN SALMON WITH DILL SAUCE

Fit for the French royal court and served as a dinner entrée for first-class passengers on the *Titanic*, poached salmon remains an incredibly moist, tender, flavorful piece of fish, cooked using a low-stress method. No surprise many fine-dining establishments around the country continue offering poached salmon on their menus, including the Golden Steer Steakhouse. The chefs at the Steer are known for a beautifully poached piece of salmon that is clean tasting and light. Just ask Holly Madison, a former Playboy bunny and now New York Times best-selling author, model, showgirl, and television personality. She's a regular guest at the Golden Steer Steakhouse, and this is her favorite dish. The secret to this recipe is to gently cook the salmon while making sure the heat doesn't get too high. A higher heat will cause drastic carryover cooking, resulting in an overcooked piece of fish.

Serves 1

- ½ cup House-Made Chicken Stock (page 69)
- ½ tablespoon Dijon mustard
- ½ teaspoon clam base
- 1 pinch white pepper
- 1 pinch fresh dill
- 1 tablespoon salted butter
- ½ lemon, juiced
- 1 8-ounce wild Alaskan salmon fillet
- 1 teaspoon Roux (page 73)

In a sauté pan over medium heat, add the chicken stock, mustard, clam base, pepper, dill, butter, and lemon juice. Whisk to combine. Add the salmon and cover, poaching in the liquid for about 3 minutes. Remove the cover and turn the fish over. Add the Roux, cover, and continue poaching for another 5 minutes. Remove from the heat and plate. Spoon the Dill Sauce over the top.

SUGGESTED PAIRING:

Mar de Frades Albarino, Rias Baixas, Spain

Mar de Frades Albarino is harvested by hand from vineyards located on the valley terraces and steep slopes of the Val do Salnes, overlooking the Atlantic Ocean. Temperature-controlled maceration and vinification of free-run must give the wine its unique freshness and aromatic intensity. Expect a green-yellow wine with golden hues and fresh primary aromas, with notes of ripe fruit and white flowers. The palate is filled with fruit, marine nuances, and good acidity, delivering an elegant freshness followed by an ample, intense finish, with lingering spicy fruit.

DOVER SOLE IN LEMON BUTTER

Serves 1

- ½ cup olive oil
- 1 extra-large (1½ pound) whole Dover sole, gutted and cleaned
- Flour, for dusting
- 1 teaspoon salted butter
- 2 teaspoons white wine
- ½ lemon, juiced
- ¼ cup House-Made Chicken Stock (page 69)
- Chopped fresh Italian parsley, for garnish

SUGGESTED PAIRING:

Nickel & Nickel Truchard Vineyard Chardonnay, Napa Valley, California

Nickel & Nickel is devoted exclusively to producing 100 percent varietal, single-vineyard wines that express the distinctive personality of each vineyard, particularly the Truchard Vineyard of Carneros, prized for its rolling hills. Established in 1997 by the partners of Far Niente, the winery is based in Oakville, California. Enjoy aromas of tropical fruits and vanilla accented by minerality in this elegant Chardonnay.

For seafood lovers, indulging at the Golden Steer Steakhouse means ordering an extra-large imported Dover sole sautéed in lemon butter and having it de-boned tableside. These true Dover sole—and there are many imposters—are caught in the icy depths of the North Sea before being shipped fresh year-round from Holland to the United States. And there's quite a demand for these tasty fish. Dover sole flesh has exceptional density, with tightly packed flakes that are juicy, buttery, and rich. This is what gives the Dover sole such exquisite flavor yet a delicate texture. To make sure you're experiencing real Dover sole like the guests at the Golden Steer Steakhouse, order your sole online from reputable seafood markets that carry the real thing. These sole are pricey compared with other flatfish, so be wary of inexpensive Dover sole or "sale" prices. And buy seafood fresh, as the Steer does, whenever possible.

Preheat the oven to 350°F.

Heat the olive oil in a large sauté pan over medium heat. Dust the sole in flour, shaking off the excess. Place it in the pan and cook until golden brown, about 2 or 3 minutes. Turn the fish over and cook the other side another 2 or 3 minutes. Drain the oil, and add to the pan the butter, white wine, lemon juice, and Chicken Stock. Place in the oven and bake for 20 to 25 minutes. Remove from the oven, arrange the fish on a serving platter, and ladle the sauce over the top. Garnish with fresh parsley and serve.

ITALIAN SPECIALTIES

Chicken of the Angels....154

Chicken Parmigiana....156

Eggplant Parmigiana....160

Veal Parmigiana....163

Veal Marsala....164

CHICKEN OF THE ANGELS

Poultry. It's a mainstay of the American diet. It's low in fat, nutritious, and a familiar protein we all know and love. One hundred years ago, chicken was more expensive than steak or lobster. Today it's one of the least expensive meats, and the boneless skinless chicken breast, featured in this prized recipe, is considered the most versatile and healthy cut. The Golden Steer Steakhouse stands for great food, great flavor, organic poultry, and sustainable farming methods. And you should, too. When selecting your chicken for this mouthwatering dish, try to purchase breasts from organic, free-range birds rather than factory-farmed birds. As one Steer chef admits, life's simply too short to drink bad wine and eat ordinary chicken.

Serves 1

- 1 tablespoon olive oil
- 1 large boneless skinless chicken breast, pounded and cut into 3 equal parts
- Flour, for dusting
- 2 eggs, whisked
- 2 whole artichoke hearts
- 2 teaspoons flour
- ½ teaspoon minced garlic
- 1 pinch white pepper
- 1 pinch dried oregano
- 1 pinch salt
- 1 pinch chopped fresh rosemary
- 4–5 large button mushrooms, sliced
- ½ cup white wine
- 1 squeezed ½ lemon
- ½ cup House-Made Chicken Stock (page 69)
- Chopped fresh Italian parsley, for garnish

Heat the olive oil in a large sauté pan over medium heat.

Dip the chicken pieces into the flour, coating all sides, and shake off the excess. Next, dip them into the egg wash, then place them into the hot pan along with the artichoke hearts. Cook until the chicken is golden brown. Flip and cook the other side until golden brown. Remove from the heat and drain the oil. Return the pan to the heat and add the additional flour, garlic, pepper, oregano, salt, rosemary, and mushrooms. Cook for 1 minute. Add the white wine, lemon juice, and House-Made Chicken Stock, and cook for an additional 5 minutes. Remove from the heat.

To serve, arrange the chicken and artichokes on a plate. Spoon the mushrooms and sauce over the top and serve with a sprinkle of parsley and a side of Wild Rice (page 192).

SUGGESTED PAIRING:

La Scolca, Gavi di Gavi Black Label, Cortese, Italy

The prestigious La Scolca Gavi dei Gavi is crafted with the utmost respect for nature, from pruning to harvesting. Strict and rigorous selection of grapes is conducted with care, cluster by cluster, in the vineyards, which are over sixty years old. Vinification is strictly traditional. The Cortese has a pale straw color, with delicate greenish highlights and an intense fruit and floral fragrance. On the palate, the wine is strongly typical of the Gavi grape: fruity and flinty with notes of almonds, hazelnuts, and walnuts lingering in the finish.

CHICKEN PARMIGIANA

Serves 4

- 2 tablespoons olive oil
- 4 boneless skinless chicken breasts, pounded thin
- Flour, for dusting
- 4 eggs, whisked
- Breadcrumbs, for coating
- 4 cups Marinara Sauce (recipe follows)
- 12 slices high-quality mozzarella cheese
- Chopped fresh Italian parsley, for garnish

What makes Italian cooking so wonderful is that most recipes only include a handful of fresh ingredients that are easily prepared. The Golden Steer Steakhouse's Chicken Parmigiana is one of these recipes. This popular dish, a variation on its deep-rooted Italian cousin, Eggplant Parmigiana (next recipe), features tender, high-quality chicken cutlets coated with bread crumbs then fried and layered with the Steer's homemade Marinara Sauce before being topped with mozzarella cheese and baked. The secret to perfecting Chicken Parmigiana is to make sure your chicken cutlets are thin and tender, and that you use a homemade sauce and not one purchased from a store. Not only does the homemade sauce taste better, but you can control the amount of salt (or sugar)—unlike the store-bought versions. Although traditional Chicken Parmigiana incorporates both mozzarella and Parmesan cheeses, Golden Steer Steakhouse chefs only use mozzarella.

Heat the olive oil in a large sauté pan over medium-low heat.

Preheat the oven to broil.

Dip each chicken breast into the flour, coating all sides, and shake off the excess. Next, dip the breasts into the egg wash, and then into the breadcrumbs. Shake off the excess and place in the hot pan. Cook until golden brown. Flip and cook the other side until golden brown and the chicken is cooked through. Remove the chicken from the pan and set aside on paper towels.

Ladle a spoonful of Marinara Sauce in the center of an ovenproof serving plate. Place one of the chicken breasts on top of the sauce. Layer another spoonful of sauce on top of the chicken, followed by three slices of mozzarella cheese. Repeat the process for the other three servings. Place the four plates under the broiler until the cheese is melted and golden brown. Remove from the oven and serve with a sprinkle of chopped parsley on top.

MARINARA SAUCE

- 1 tablespoon olive oil
- 5 fresh basil leaves, chopped
- 1 teaspoon minced garlic
- 1 pinch white pepper
- 1 pinch dried chicken base
- 1 pinch dried oregano
- 5 cups tomato puree
- 1 tablespoon white wine

For home cooks, try the chicken base from Better Than Bouillon (available at most markets and online), made from chicken meat and natural chicken juices.

Heat the olive oil in a stockpot over medium heat. Add the basil, garlic, pepper, chicken base, oregano, and tomato puree. Stir well, and let the mixture cook for about 5 minutes. Add the white wine and reduce the heat to low. Simmer for about 10 minutes, stirring occasionally.

SUGGESTED PAIRING:

Tenuta di Arceno, Il Fauno di Arcanum, Italy

The Jackson family purchased the Tenuta di Arceno estate in 1994, with its sprawling 2,500 acres, of which only 223 are planted to vine. Cabernet Franc has proven to be the variety best suited to the estate's diverse soils and topography; it's the true signature of the estate, as it thrives in both warm and cool vintages. One of the more complex and elegant in many vintages, Il Fauno is a Super Tuscan Blend that presents floral aromas of fresh-cut roses and beautifully ripe strawberries. On the palate soft, velvety, structured tannins make way for rich plum and candied cherries, with nutmeg and black licorice undertones. A vibrant acidity prolongs the finish with lingering notes of sweet cedar and tobacco.

EGGPLANT PARMIGIANA

Serves 4

- 2 tablespoons olive oil
- 4 thick slices from a large eggplant
- Flour, for dusting
- 4 eggs, whisked
- Breadcrumbs, for coating
- 4 cups Marinara Sauce (page 157)
- 8 slices mozzarella cheese
- Chopped fresh Italian parsley, for garnish

This dish represents classic southern Italian cuisine with sliced eggplant (first cultivated in China before being introduced to Italy in the fourteenth century) taking center stage. Eggplant, incidentally, belongs to the same plant family as tomatoes and bell peppers, and is loaded with vitamins and minerals, as well as antioxidants. This recipe is prepared essentially the same way as Chicken Parmigiana, with the only difference being that the Golden Steer Steakhouse serves this entrée with two slices of melted mozzarella cheese instead of three. When selecting an eggplant, make sure you pick one that is firm and heavy for its size, with skin that's smooth and free from discoloration and bruises.

Heat the olive oil in a large sauté pan over medium-low heat.

Preheat the oven to broil.

Dip each eggplant slice into the flour, coating all sides, and shake off the excess. Next, dip the slices into the egg wash, and then into the breadcrumbs. Shake off the excess and place in the hot pan. Cook for 2 or 3 minutes. Flip and cook the other side for another 3 or 4 minutes. Remove the eggplant from the pan and set aside on paper towels.

Ladle a spoonful of Marinara Sauce in the center of each ovenproof serving plate. Place an eggplant slice on top of the sauce. Layer another spoonful of sauce on top of the eggplant, followed by two slices of mozzarella cheese. Repeat the process for the other three servings. Place the four plates under the broiler until the cheese is melted and golden brown. Remove from the oven and serve with a sprinkle of chopped parsley on top.

SUGGESTED PAIRING:

Lamole di Lamole Chianti Classico, Sangiovese, Italy

One of the most important wine regions in Italy, Tuscany is home to the cities of Florence and Siena, the districts of Chianti and Brunello di Montalcino, and the wineries of Sassicaia, Tignanello, and Ornellaia. Tuscany is also home to the indigenous Italian grape variety Sangiovese. Deep ruby red, this Sangiovese features black cherry and forest fruit fragrances along with flower-like aromatics, a roundness mid-palate, and a finish with fruit and spice sweetness.

VEAL PARMIGIANA

Made in the same manner as the Eggplant Parmigiana, Veal Parmigiana is included in this chapter because, yes, it's delicious, and also because the Golden Steer Steakhouse is aware of veal's questionable public reputation. You'll be glad to know Steer chefs purchase tender, juicy, sweet-tasting veal from reputable veal farmers who are committed to ensuring the health and well-being of their calves while taking care of the environment and providing safe, high-quality, nutritious food for consumers. Most of these farmers operate in the Midwest and Northeast, where they raise their veal calves on small family farms and follow the ethical standards and code of conduct set forth by the US veal industry. Now you can enjoy this delicious dish and appreciate its flavors without the guilt.

Serves 4

- 2 tablespoons olive oil
- 4 veal cutlets, pounded thin
- Flour, for dusting
- 4 eggs, whisked
- Breadcrumbs, for coating
- 4 cups Marinara Sauce (page 157)
- 8 slices mozzarella cheese
- Chopped fresh Italian parsley, for garnish

Heat the olive oil in a large sauté pan over medium-low heat.

Preheat the oven to broil.

Dip each veal cutlet into the flour, coating all sides, and shake off the excess. Next, dip the cutlets into the egg wash, and then into the breadcrumbs. Shake off the excess and place in the hot pan. Cook for 2 minutes. Flip and cook the other side until it reaches your desired internal temperature. Remove the cutlets from the pan and set aside on paper towels.

Ladle a spoonful of Marinara Sauce in the center of an ovenproof serving plate. Place one veal cutlet on top of the sauce. Layer another spoonful of sauce on top of the cutlet, followed by two slices of mozzarella cheese. Repeat the process for the other three servings. Place the four plates under the broiler until the cheese is melted and golden brown. Remove from the oven and serve with a sprinkle of chopped parsley on top.

SUGGESTED PAIRING:

Masi Costasera Amarone Classico, Veneto, Italy

Costasera's slopes face the sunset, making this the best terroir for producing high-quality Amarone in Valpolicella Classico. With a longer day, vines that face Lake Garda bask in reflected light, receiving more sunshine. Masi combines ancient varieties (Corvina, Rondinella, and Molinara) and winemaking methods (vinifying grapes semi-dried on racks for three to four months) with the latest techniques: Bamboo racks in temperature- and humidity-controlled conditions induce natural drying. This deep ruby-red wine has powerful, complex aromas of dried plums and balsamic (anise, fennel, mint) traces. Quite dry (not sweet) on the palate, soft and with bright acidity, the wine shows flavors of baked cherry, chocolate, and cinnamon. Structured but noble, delicate tannins precede a long finish.

VEAL MARSALA

Serves 1

- 1 tablespoon olive oil
- 4 large veal medallions, pounded
- Flour, for dusting
- 1 teaspoon flour
- ½ teaspoon minced garlic
- 1 pinch white pepper
- 1 pinch dried oregano
- 1 pinch salt
- ½ tablespoon salted butter
- 4–5 large button mushrooms, sliced
- ¼ cup Marsala wine
- ½ cup House-Made Beef Stock (page 68)
- 1 cup cooked Wild Rice (page 192)
- Chopped fresh Italian parsley, for garnish

SUGGESTED PAIRING:

Terra di Trulli Pinnacoli, Primitivo di Manduria, Puglia, Italy

Trulli are ancient stone dwellings with cone-shaped roofs found only in the magnificent Puglia region of southern Italy. At the pinnacle of the cone roofs sit magical symbols of good fortune known as pinnacoli. Pinnacoli Primitivo is the pinnacle of this classic grape varietal, full-bodied with rich, concentrated fruit flavors. A ruby-red wine with full flavors of ripe red fruits and a hint of spice, Pinnacoli has flavors of wild strawberry through the palate, and finishes with a rich fullness with hints of cinnamon.

Veal Marsala, another classic Italian veal dish, dates back to the nineteenth century, particularly in Sicily where Marsala wine is produced. It features naturally tender cutlets with delicate flavor and little fat, which gets infused with sweet Italian Marsala wine. Because the veal in this dish is also pounded thin, the medallions only require brief sautéing on each side, often one or two minutes—just enough to add a golden-brown coating and to warm the meat before it's returned to the pan.

Heat the olive oil in a large sauté pan over medium heat.

Dip the veal medallions into the flour, coating all sides, and shake off the excess (note: if you find the medallions too large, you can cut them into smaller pieces). Place in the hot pan and cook until golden brown. Flip and cook the other side until golden brown. Remove from the heat and drain the oil. Return the pan to the heat and add the flour, garlic, pepper, oregano, salt, butter, and mushrooms. Cook for 1 minute. Add the Marsala wine and House-Made Beef Stock, and cook for an additional 5 minutes.

To serve, spoon a layer of Wild Rice on a serving plate. Arrange the veal medallions on top of the rice. Spoon the mushrooms and sauce over the veal and serve with a sprinkle of parsley on top.

VINTAGE SELECTIONS

Fresh Brook Trout....170

Baked Halibut Piccante....172

Scallops Piccante....173

Frog Legs in Garlic Butter....175

Broiled Half Chicken....176

Bob White Quail with Wild Rice....178

FRESH BROOK TROUT

Brook trout, a popular game fish with fly fishers, is a beautiful North American trout with a dark-green to brown color and a distinctive marbled pattern. In nature, they are found in cold, clean creeks, rivers, and lakes. They are also raised commercially for human consumption. Today more than seventy million pounds of trout, mostly rainbow trout, are grown annually in the United States, and are available year-round. The trout you find at the market is all farm-raised, but still delicious. The meat is mild, delicate, sweet, and good for you. Trout, like salmon, contains omega-3, which helps reduce heart disease and lower cholesterol. This dinner special from the Golden Steer Steakhouse Vintage Selections menu is served with soup or salad, along with the Steer's famous Garlic Bread.

Serves 2

- ¼ cup olive oil
- 2 whole fresh brook (or rainbow) trout (about 1 pound each), cleaned, butterflied, head still intact
- Flour, for dusting
- 1 tablespoon salted butter
- 1 tablespoon white wine
- ½ lemon, juiced
- 1 tablespoon House-Made Chicken Stock (page 69)
- Chopped fresh Italian parsley, for garnish

Preheat the oven to 350°F.

Heat the olive oil in a large sauté pan over medium heat. Dust both sides of the trout in flour, shaking off the excess. Place in the pan and cook until one side is golden brown. Turn the fish over and place directly in the oven for 7 or 8 minutes. Remove from the oven and drain the oil. Set back over medium heat and add the butter, white wine, lemon juice, and Chicken Stock. Cook for 1 or 2 minutes, until the liquid is the consistency of a creamy sauce. Remove from the heat. Arrange the trout on a serving platter and spoon the sauce over the top. Garnish with parsley and serve.

SUGGESTED PAIRING:

King Estate Pinot Noir, Willamette Valley, Oregon

One of the best-known bottlings of Pinot Noir in America, organically grown Pinot Noir from the King Estate vineyard is blended with grapes from sustainably farmed vineyards throughout Oregon. The palate offers an elegant blend of dark cherries, rhubarb, and blackberry, evolving into complex flavors of cranberry, walnut, and cassis.

SCALLOPS PICCANTE

Unlike the Halibut Piccante, this piccante dish from the Golden Steer Steakhouse does include a hot, spicy ingredient—red pepper flakes. Made in a similar fashion, this dinner entrée can be served with either large day-boat diver scallops or the smaller bay scallops. If you're using bay scallops, consider about one pound for two servings. A quick note on scallops: Whenever possible, purchase dry scallops as opposed to wet scallops. Wet scallops are often treated with a "soapy" preserving solution and then frozen, whereas dry scallops are not preserved, offering a much fresher-tasting, sweeter scallop.

Serves 1 or 2

- ¼ tablespoon olive oil
- 6 large day-boat diver scallops
- 3–4 white mushrooms, cleaned and sliced
- 1 tablespoon salted butter
- ½ teaspoon minced garlic
- 1 pinch salt
- 1 pinch white pepper
- 1 pinch oregano
- 1 pinch crushed red pepper flakes
- 2–3 dashes Worcestershire sauce
- ½ lemon, juiced
- 1 teaspoon Roux (page 73)
- ¼ cup House-Made Chicken Stock (page 69)
- 1/2 tablespoon white wine
- Chopped fresh Italian parsley, for garnish

Heat the olive oil in a large sauté pan over medium heat. Add the scallops and mushrooms to the pan and cook for about 2 minutes. Turn the scallops and mushrooms over and remove from the heat. Drain the oil, and return the pan to the heat. Add the butter, garlic, salt, pepper, oregano, red pepper flakes, Worcestershire, lemon juice, and Roux. Stir well to combine. Add the Chicken Stock and white wine. Continue to cook for about 5 minutes, or until the scallops are cooked through and the liquid is the consistency of a creamy sauce. Remove from the heat. Transfer the scallops to a serving platter and ladle the mushrooms and sauce over the top. Garnish with parsley and serve.

SUGGESTED PAIRING:

Sonoma-Cutrer Vineyards Chardonnay, Russian River Valley, California

Russian River Ranches is a cuvée of distinct vineyard lots, each contributing its own personality to the wine. These vineyards come together to create a Chardonnay that is consistent from year to year and remains among the most coveted in each and every vintage. True to the Russian River Ranches style, this wine is beautifully focused with a nice, bright acidity balanced by a long finish and a light mid-palate creaminess. It's fruit-forward, loaded with aromas of lemon and lime, and accented with nougat, green apple, spices, pear, and touches of wet stone minerality. Crisp and zesty flavors of lemon drop, green apple, white peach, and lychee are accented with a nice barrel spice and persistent lime.

FROG LEGS IN GARLIC BUTTER

Believe it or not, frog legs were once so sought after that many frog species almost became extinct. From the Catholic Church in France (believed to be responsible for adding frog legs to French cuisine) to the California gold miners who nearly extirpated the California red-legged frog, the hunt for frog legs was fierce. Today most of the frog legs served are farmed. The two most popular varieties are the American bullfrog and the southern leopard frog. When selecting frog legs to prepare, whether they're wild or farmed, look for big, meaty legs, which are rich in protein, omega-3, vitamin A, and potassium. Unfortunately, the Golden Steer Steakhouse no longer serves frog legs to their guests.

Serves 1 or 2

- 1 tablespoon olive oil
- 6 large frog legs, skinned and split in half
- Flour, for dusting
- ½ tablespoon salted butter
- ½ teaspoon minced garlic
- 1 pinch salt
- 1 pinch white pepper
- 1 pinch oregano
- ½ tablespoon white wine
- ½ lemon, juiced
- 1 tablespoon House-Made Chicken Stock (page 69)
- 1 teaspoon Roux (page 73)
- Chopped fresh Italian parsley, for garnish

Heat the olive oil in a large sauté pan over medium heat. Dust both sides of the frog legs in flour, shaking off the excess. Place in the pan and cook until one side is golden brown. Remove from the heat and drain the oil. Return the pan to the heat and turn the frog legs over. Add the butter, garlic, salt, pepper, oregano, white wine, lemon juice, Chicken Stock, and Roux. Stir well to combine. Continue to cook until the legs are cooked through and the liquid is the consistency of a creamy sauce. Remove from the heat. Transfer the frog legs to a serving platter and ladle the sauce over the top. Garnish with parsley and serve.

SUGGESTED PAIRING:

J. J. Vincent, Pouilly-Fuissé Cuvée Marie Antoinette, Chardonnay, Burgundy, France

Maison J. J. Vincent produces a range of wines made with the same care and expertise as those made at the Vincents' historic domaine, Château Fuissé. This Chardonnay is made from grapes sourced from Mâconnais and cru Beaujolais vineyards owned by other members of Jean-Jacques Vincent's family. The wine is pale yellow in color with hints of green. A touch of oak, lots of finesse, and minerality with white flower, lemon, and apple scents adds to its depth. Overall, the wine is nicely balanced and fresh with a great length.

BROILED HALF CHICKEN

Serves 1

- 1 tablespoon olive oil
- ½ spring chicken
- 1 cup cooked Wild Rice (page 192)
- Chopped fresh Italian parsley, for garnish

It doesn't get any more simple and delicious than chicken and rice. This was a huge seller during the golden era of the Golden Steer Steakhouse. Today serving a spring chicken—another term for a young chicken (two to three months old) that weighs around a pound and a half to two pounds—might be a little difficult: Many markets no longer sell old-style spring chickens, sometimes referred to as broilers. If you do find one, there's a good chance the bird will weigh over two pounds given today's expansive poultry industry and a selective breeding process that makes chickens grow a lot faster and heavier than they used to. This is one of the reasons this dish slowly disappeared from the Golden Steer Steakhouse menu.

Preheat the oven to 350°F.

Add the oil to a sauté pan along with the chicken. Place in the oven and cook until the chicken is cooked through, about 20 minutes. Remove the pan from the oven and transfer the chicken to a serving plate along with the Wild Rice. Garnish with parsley and serve.

SUGGESTED PAIRING:

Bodegas Faustino I Gran Reserva,
Tempranillo, Spain

Bodegas Faustino is Rioja's largest exporter of Gran Reserva wines. The winner of numerous awards and gold medals in international competitions and tastings, Bodegas Faustino is a proud custodian of the Rioja region's growing international reputation as a source of truly world-class fine wines. This Tempranillo is aromatic and complex, with notes of tobacco, cedar, and leather against a background of ripe fruit, jam, and spices with flavors of rich red fruit, licorice, and minerals as well as smooth, ripe tannins.

BOB WHITE QUAIL WITH WILD RICE

Serves 1

- 2 teaspoons olive oil
- 2 quail, cleaned
- 1 cup cooked Wild Rice (page 192)
- 2 tablespoons Peppercorn Sauce (page 198)
- Chopped fresh Italian parsley, for garnish

This gourmet special offered at the Golden Steer Steakhouse featured two quails served on a bed of Wild Rice. Accompanying sides included Hearts of Palm with a vinaigrette dressing, fresh vegetables drizzled with Hollandaise, and your choice of dessert and coffee or tea. The Steer also paired quail with either an Australian lobster tail or a filet mignon. If quail wasn't your thing, you could also order pheasant, chukkars, or a guinea hen, although these game birds required twenty-four hours' advance notice. The Steer's Bob White Quail (the correct spelling is *bobwhite quail*, but it's written as Bob White Quail on the old menu) is a moderate-sized quail and the most common species of quail in America. Though you don't typically see them offered every day in American markets, farm-raised quail can be ordered easily from various farms with a few days' notice. An important note worth mentioning: Wild game birds can no longer be served in restaurants or sold in retail markets unless they have been slaughtered and dressed under USDA or equivalent foreign inspection.

Preheat the oven to 350°F.

Add the oil to a sauté pan along with the quail. Place in the oven and cook until the quail is cooked through, about 10 minutes. Remove from the oven. Arrange the Wild Rice in the center of a serving plate and place the quail on top. Drizzle the Peppercorn Sauce over the top. Garnish with parsley and serve.

SUGGESTED PAIRING:

Casa Lapostolle Grand Selection, Carménère, Rapel Valley, Chile

Lapostolle was founded by Alexandra Marnier Lapostolle and her husband, Cyril de Bournet, in 1994. The Marnier Lapostolle family, founders and owners of the world-renowned liqueur Grand Marnier, is famous for producing spirits and liqueurs, but the family has also been involved in winemaking for generations. Medium-bodied with intense, inky violet color, their Carménère releases aromas of leather, dark fruit, coffee, and chocolate. Flavors of cassis, cherry plum, pepper, earthy nuances, vanilla, and spice round out the wine.

ACCOMPANIMENTS, SIDES & SAUCES

Sautéed Mushrooms.....187

Fresh Vegetables.....188

Creamed Spinach.....189

Creamed Corn.....190

Wild Rice.....192

Jumbo Baked Potato.....193

Twice-Baked Potato.....194

Whipped Potatoes.....196

Fresh-Cut Steak Fries.....197

Peppercorn Sauce.....198

Hollandaise Sauce.....200

Béarnaise Sauce.....201

SAUTÉED MUSHROOMS

The Golden Steer Steakhouse prides itself on serving incredibly easy and savory side dishes to accompany their outstanding entrées, and these Sautéed Mushrooms are no exception. Steer chefs prefer using large cultivated white mushrooms for this dish, but feel free to experiment with other edible types. If you're not familiar with how to properly wash mushrooms, make sure to never soak them or run them under water. Mushrooms are like a sponge, and will absorb the water, causing your perfect sauté to be watered down and soggy. Instead, use damp paper towels or a pastry brush to clean off any excess dirt. This simple step will allow your clean, dry mushrooms to absorb the tasty sauce you've prepared and not the water they were cleaned in.

Serves 2

- 1 tablespoon olive oil
- 10 large cultivated white mushrooms, washed (never soaked)
- ½ teaspoon minced garlic
- 1 pinch salt
- 1 pinch white pepper
- 1 pinch oregano
- 1 tablespoon salted butter
- ½ teaspoon Roux (page 73)
- 1 tablespoon white wine
- 1 tablespoon House-Made Chicken Stock (page 69)
- Chopped fresh Italian (flat-leaf) parsley, for garnish

Heat the olive oil in a large sauté pan over medium heat. Add the mushrooms, garlic, salt, pepper, oregano, butter, Roux, white wine, and Chicken Stock. Mix well to combine. Cook until the mushrooms are soft but still hold their shape, about 5 to 8 minutes. Remove from the heat. Arrange the mushrooms on a side dish, ladle the sauce over the top, garnish with parsley, and serve.

FRESH VEGETABLES

Number of servings depends on how many vegetables are being cooked

- Fresh asparagus
- Fresh broccoli
- Fresh carrots, peeled and sliced on the bias, about ½ inch thick
- ¼ teaspoon baking soda

Fresh-cooked asparagus, broccoli, and carrots are what's served at the Golden Steer Steakhouse, but feel free to incorporate other vegetables into your menu. The trick to perfect-looking cooked vegetables is adding just a touch of baking soda to the water. Baking soda helps maintain the vegetables' vivid colors, but adding too much will ruin them, too. That's because baking soda, added in large amounts, will break down the cell walls of the vegetables, causing them to become mushy. Too much baking soda can also destroy vegetables' important vitamins, particularly vitamin C and thiamin. All you need is a very small pinch to keep your cooked vegetables looking their best.

Fill a stockpot with water and set it over high heat. Bring to a boil. Add the vegetables and baking soda, and boil, about 10 minutes. The vegetables should be bright in color, and not soft or mushy. Remove from the heat and drain the water, leaving the vegetables in the pot. Immediately fill the pot with cold running water. Let the cold water continue to circulate into the pot of vegetables for about 10 minutes. Drain the cold water, and reserve the vegetables until ready to use. To reheat, simply add the vegetables to a pot of hot (not boiling) water for 4 to 5 minutes.

CREAMED SPINACH

The cooking process for Creamed Spinach is virtually the same as for Creamed Corn. This was a favorite dish of the great Muhammad Ali, a frequent guest at the Golden Steer Steakhouse. In fact, before Ali celebrated his seventieth birthday in front of more than two thousand people at a red carpet gala at the MGM Grand in Las Vegas, the champ had a quiet dinner with family and friends at the Golden Steer.

Serves 4

- 1½ cups frozen chopped spinach
- ½ cup heavy cream
- ½ teaspoon minced garlic
- 1 teaspoon minced shallots
- 1 tablespoon salted butter
- 1 teaspoon Pernod
- 1 tablespoon fresh-grated Parmesan cheese
- 2 teaspoons Roux (page 73)

In a small stockpot over low heat, add the spinach, heavy cream, garlic, shallots, butter, and Pernod. Mix well to combine. Let simmer for about 15 minutes, stirring occasionally. Remove from the heat, stir in the Parmesan and Roux, and keep warm until ready to serve.

CREAMED CORN

Serves 4

- 2 cups fresh corn kernels
- 1 cup heavy cream
- 1 teaspoon minced garlic
- 1 teaspoon minced shallots
- 1 pinch white pepper
- ¼ teaspoon ground nutmeg
- 2 tablespoons sugar
- 1 tablespoon Roux (page 73)

Sweet corn is delicious, of course, but sweet corn simmered in a bath of cream and spices, well, that's another heaven entirely. In keeping with tradition, Golden Steer Steakhouse chefs don't serve their Creamed Corn until it's been perfectly simmered on the stovetop and every kernel is plump with cream and coated with sauce. Another secret to the Steer's incredible Creamed Corn is the addition of ground nutmeg, which brings the perfect warmth of spicy sweet flavor. Whenever possible, freshly grind your nutmeg directly from the seed rather than using the pre-ground store-bought nutmeg in a jar. The flavor is far superior.

In a small stockpot over low heat, add the corn, heavy cream, garlic, shallots, pepper, nutmeg, sugar, and Roux. Mix well to combine. Let simmer for about 30 minutes, stirring occasionally. Remove from the heat and keep warm until ready to serve.

WILD RICE

Serves 2–4

- 4½ cups cold water
- 1½ cups long-grain wild rice
- Salt and white pepper, to taste

Wild rice is an ancient grain that has been harvested for thousands of years, from the Chinese to the Native Americans. Today wild rice is also cultivated, which is less expensive and more widely available than truly wild rice, which is often known as "organic" wild rice, even though it's not certified organic because it's foraged in the wild. True wild rice is expensive because it requires precise conditions for growth. The Golden Steer Steakhouse uses true wild rice, which is rich in nutrients, low in fat, and contains no gluten. Keep in mind that wild rice takes longer to cook than regular rice, and it helps to soak the rice overnight before cooking, which renders it more digestible. The long straight grains of truly wild rice have a deep, earthy, and nutty fragrance and flavor, and the Steer chefs admit it's well worth the higher cost.

In a medium saucepot, bring the water to a boil over high heat. Add the rice and return to a boil. Cover, reduce the heat to a simmer, and cook until the rice is tender, about 40 to 50 minutes. Drain the rice, season with salt and white pepper, and keep warm until ready to serve.

JUMBO BAKED POTATO

The following four potato sides, all prepared and served at the Golden Steer Steakhouse, begin with large two-pound Idaho russet potatoes. Although russet potatoes are grown in many states, only russet potatoes grown in Idaho can be called Idaho russet potatoes. So what makes these particular potatoes so special? Idaho's perfect growing conditions, which include the rich, volcanic soil and the unique climate and irrigation. The result is a very large potato that has a high solid content, meaning there's more potato and less water. To make sure you're buying genuine, top-quality Idaho russet potatoes, look for those with the GROWN IN IDAHO seal

Number of servings depends on how many potatoes are being baked

- Large Idaho russet potato (about 2 pounds each)
- Condiments: crumbled bacon, fresh chives, sour cream, cheddar cheese, salt, white pepper

---

Preheat the oven to 350°F.

Place the potato (or potatoes) on a baking sheet and set in the oven (do not wrap in foil; baking directly in the oven allows for a nice, crispy skin). Bake for about 2 hours, or until cooked through and soft. Serve with your chosen condiments.

TWICE-BAKED POTATO

Serves 1

- 1 Jumbo Baked Potato (previous recipe)
- 1 tablespoon crumbled cooked bacon
- 1 tablespoon sour cream
- 1 teaspoon chopped fresh chives
- ½ tablespoon fresh-grated cheddar cheese
- 1 tablespoon melted salted butter
- 1 pinch white pepper
- 1 pinch paprika

Preheat the oven to 350°F.

Split the Jumbo Baked Potato in half. Remove as much of the potato as you can from both halves, being careful not to split or damage the skin. Place the potato in a mixing bowl and add the bacon, sour cream, chives, cheddar, melted butter, and pepper. Use a potato masher to mash the ingredients until smooth. Scoop the mixture back into one of the skins. (Note: If there is enough mixture left over, fill the other skin, but typically this makes enough to fill just one of the skin halves.) Score the top of the stuffing in a crosshatched pattern using the back of a knife. Sprinkle with paprika and bake for 10 minutes.

WHIPPED POTATOES

Number of servings depends on how many potatoes are used

- Large Idaho russet potatoes (about 2 pounds each)
- Salt
- White pepper
- Salted butter
- Fresh-grated Parmesan cheese
- Heavy cream

Fill a stockpot with water and set it over high heat. Bring to a boil.

Peel the potatoes and slice them. Add them to the boiling water and boil until they're tender. Drain the water completely, leaving the potatoes in the pot. Add the salt, pepper, butter, Parmesan, and heavy cream. Whisk vigorously until the potatoes are light and fluffy. Keep warm until ready to serve.

FRESH-CUT STEAK FRIES

Number of servings depends on how many potatoes are used

- Canola oil, for deep-frying
- Large Idaho russet potatoes (about 2 pounds each)

Heat the oil in a deep fryer, or use a large wok or stockpot filled halfway with oil.

Peel the potatoes, then remove both ends from each. Run them through a french fry press—or you can simply use a sharp kitchen knife to slice them into wedges or steak fries, 4 or 5 inches long, and ½ inch thick.

Working in batches, carefully add the potatoes to the hot oil and deep-fry until golden brown. Remove from the oil and drain. Serve warm.

PEPPERCORN SAUCE

Makes about 2 cups

- 1 tablespoon olive oil
- ½ teaspoon minced garlic
- ¼ teaspoon white pepper
- ½ cup House-Made Chicken Stock (page 69)
- ½ cup House-Made Beef Stock (page 68)
- ½ teaspoon A-1 Steak Sauce
- 1 tablespoon ketchup
- 1 tablespoon Heinz 57 Sauce
- ½ teaspoon Worcestershire sauce
- 1 tablespoon red wine vinegar
- 1 tablespoon black peppercorns, roughly crushed
- ¼ cup finely chopped button mushrooms
- ¼ cup finely chopped celery
- ¼ cup finely chopped white onion
- ½ tablespoon Roux (page 73)

A favorite sauce of race car legend Mario Andretti, a frequent guest at the Golden Steer Steakhouse, this creamy reduction is perfect atop a grilled steak, particularly filet mignon. Although you can use different types of peppercorns, such as green or pink, Steer chefs prefer using black peppercorns, primarily for their distinct flavor and appearance in the sauce. For the veal demi-glace, there are many high-quality brands on the market, including Williams-Sonoma and D'Artagnan, which contain no fat, salt, or preservatives.

In a sauté pan over low heat, add the olive oil, garlic, white pepper, House-Made Chicken Stock, House-Made Beef Stock, A-1 Steak Sauce, ketchup, Heinz 57 Sauce, Worcestershire, red wine vinegar, and the black peppercorns. Whisk to combine. Add the chopped mushrooms, celery and onion, and continue whisking. Allow the sauce to simmer over low heat. Add the Roux to thicken the sauce, and whisk occasionally, for about 10 minutes. Remove from the heat and serve warm in a gravy boat.

HOLLANDAISE SAUCE

Makes about 2 cups

- 5 egg yolks
- 1 teaspoon warm water
- 1 pinch salt
- 1 pinch white pepper
- 2–3 dashes Tabasco hot sauce
- 2 cups melted salted butter
- 1 lemon, juiced

A lusciously rich, lemony, buttery sauce, Hollandaise is best spooned over vegetables, like asparagus, and various seafood dishes, while Béarnaise is generally reserved for beef, although the Golden Steer Steakhouse's Filet Mignon Oscar-Style calls for Hollandaise. Developed in the 1600s in the Netherlands and France, Hollandaise does require a little experience and skill to master because of the addition of egg yolks, which you don't want to separate. Although there are Hollandaise dry mixes available on the market, to which you simply add water or milk, make your Hollandaise—and all the sauces in this book, for that matter—from scratch whenever possible. The end result will be well worth your time.

In a small stockpot, add the egg yolks, warm water, salt, pepper, and Tabasco. Whisk well to combine and place over low heat. Slowly whisk in the melted butter and lemon juice. Continue whisking until the sauce thickens, about 5 minutes. Remove from the heat and serve in a gravy boat.

BÉARNAISE SAUCE

If you are able to make the previous Hollandaise Sauce from scratch, you'll have no problem making the Golden Steer Steakhouse's Béarnaise Sauce, as it's virtually identical; the only difference is the addition of dried tarragon leaves.

Makes about 2 cups

- 5 egg yolks
- 1 teaspoon warm water
- 1 pinch salt
- 1 pinch white pepper
- 2–3 dashes Tabasco hot sauce
- 2 cups melted salted butter
- 1 lemon, juiced
- 2 teaspoons dried tarragon leaves

In a small stockpot, add the egg yolks, warm water, salt, pepper, and Tabasco. Whisk well to combine and place over low heat. Slowly whisk in the melted butter, lemon juice, and tarragon leaves. Continue whisking until the sauce thickens, about 5 minutes. Remove from the heat and serve in a gravy boat.

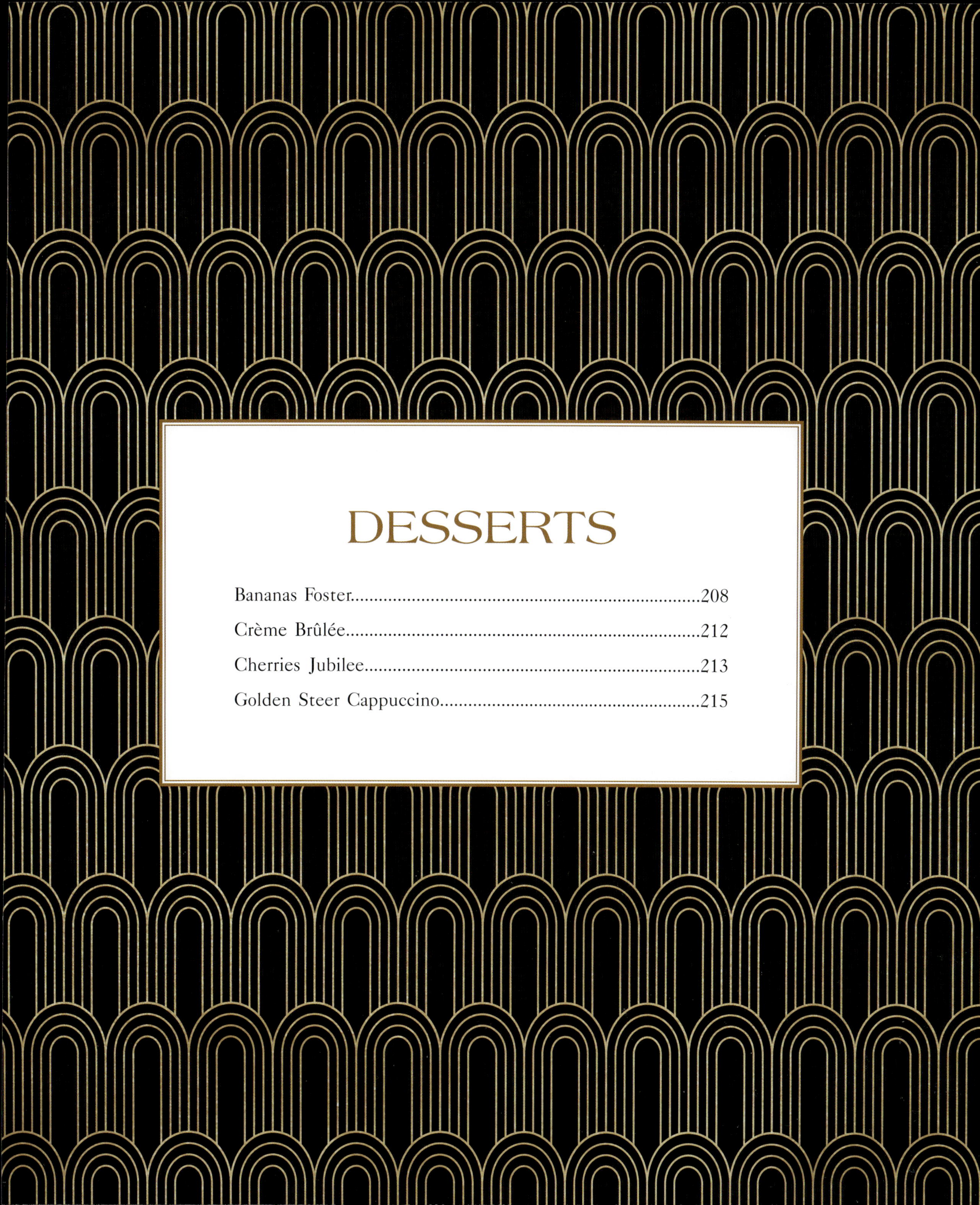

DESSERTS

Bananas Foster....208

Crème Brûlée....212

Cherries Jubilee....213

Golden Steer Cappuccino....215

BANANAS FOSTER

Serves 1 or 2

- 1 tablespoon salted butter
- 1 tablespoon brown sugar
- 1 tablespoon crème de banana
- ½ teaspoon fresh lemon zest
- 1 fresh orange (1 teaspoon orange zest and 1 tablespoon orange juice)
- 1 large ripe banana, peeled and cut into ½-inch slices
- 1 splash Bacardi Rum 151
- 2–3 dashes cinnamon (optional)
- 1 cup (2–3 scoops) vanilla ice cream

The Golden Steer Steakhouse is of course famous in its own right, but this decadent dessert, along with Cherries Jubilee, is equally famous. Prepared and flambéed tableside in front of guests, Bananas Foster and Cherries Jubilee are the only two desserts assembled not by the chefs, but by the Steer servers themselves. Without question, this sweet indulgence is an impressive and mouthwatering surprise for your next dinner party, family gathering, or special celebration. Just ask actor Nicolas Cage, who likes to take it one step further by ordering the Bananas Foster ingredients from the Golden Steer Steakhouse, so he can assemble the iconic dessert at home. Other celebrities and regular guests at the Steer who often request the Bananas Foster, but elect to have it made in front of them, include legendary race car driver Mario Andretti and former Playboy bunny Holly Madison. This was also Frank Sinatra's favorite dessert at the Golden Steer Steakhouse. It should be pointed out that the addition of cinnamon is only used for the tableside theatrics, as the spice, when ignited, creates a dazzling array of sparks. If you prefer to forgo the sparks, simply omit the cinnamon.

Melt the butter in a sauté pan over medium heat. Add the brown sugar, crème de banana, lemon zest, orange zest, and orange juice. Stir frequently and reduce the mixture until it's caramelized; don't allow it to burn. Add the banana slices in an even layer, coating them with the sauce. Add a splash of Bacardi Rum 151, and continue to cook for about 1½ minutes. Add the dashes of cinnamon, if desired. Remove from the heat and serve immediately atop vanilla ice cream in a chilled bowl.

SUGGESTED PAIRING:

Graham's 20 Year Old Tawny Port

W & J Graham's was founded in Porto in 1820. Renowned worldwide for outstanding vintage ports, Graham's also produces a range of aged tawny, late-bottled vintage, reserve, and Quinta dos Malvedos vintage ports. This port blend showcases a golden tawny color and a flavor redolent of nuts, such as almonds, and delicious mature fruit with hints of orange peel. Rich, sweet, and smooth on the palate, the port is perfectly balanced with a long and lingering finish.

RUM